i

BILL & I

*Building William Shatner's
Belle Reve Ranch*

*By
Dalan E. Smith*

DEDICATION

—————— • ——————

To Judith Nell Smith, my wife, the love of my life; the one that brought me to Three Rivers and this adventure, as well as other great adventures of our time together.

ACKNOWLEDGMENTS

The most gratitude goes to my wife, Judy, as she has put up with me and my desires to read and write incessantly for all these years, and still does. Writing coaches Christina Lynch and Bill Haxton have provided suggestions of help and encouragement, and have kept me motivated long enough to complete this project. Daughter Terry Stewart acted capably as the main proofreader, daughter Carolyn Barton stored backup copies and offered encouragement. Other children, Chris Smith and Kristi Tilchen, were constant cheerleaders and helped me organize thoughts. Special thanks to Tom and Dodie Marshall of the Three Rivers Historical Society for information on the flood of 1867. Others instrumental in keeping me in motion on this project include my friends and fellow authors, Betty Luceigh and Ned Pinhey, and those around me upon whom I still inflict my enthusiasm for writing.

CONTENTS

INTRODUCTION

●

This is a journey of my soul, mostly autobiographical, but containing views of William Shatner seen only by those closely associated with him, views of the gentle side of the man who played the "Captain Kirk" character, including stories of his private life on his very private foothill quarter horse ranch. It also defines how my psyche operates and grows (or regresses) as I experience new and different events than I had ever imagined I would, and defines how the immensely strong bonds of love and loving family can see us through any trouble we encounter, regardless of our station in life. Hope is real; hope that the future will outperform the past can bring us to levels of personal performance that we didn't know existed. After all, what is life for if not to grow, to increase in our capacities? Looking in detail at the lives, successes, failures, strengths, foibles, and journeys of others, especially the successful, can be not just enjoyable, but also really instructional for the mind ready to expand and grow into potentials previously not recognized.

As I look back at one of my seven decades and what transpired there, I become better at seeing why I so enjoy looking at others and trying to decide what makes them what they are, and watching how our individual attitudes shape our personalities. It was during this decade that I fell into an opportunity to study up close a member of the celebrity class, something I had never seriously done before, or even thought I might enjoy. As my wife, Judy, and I became acquainted with William Shatner, whom I had previously known only as a fan of his role as Captain Kirk, I found a great chance to get a glimpse of a personality in a stratum of human existence of which I had absolutely no experience. I had never spent a lot of time watching movies or television, but had seen and enjoyed some of the Star Trek series episodes. There had been no opportunity in my growing up in rural Idaho to meet or know any celebrities, and starting a family while in college then immediately immersing myself in a corporate career pretty much limited my time to do social things, even if I had moved in the circles these people frequented.

We became associated with Bill, as he preferred to be called, after I had experienced enough of the corporate climbing scene and desired a lower profile for myself, and our respect for his desires for privacy kept me from taking advantage of that celebrity status to further any latent longings I may have had for fame or recognition. Now, some thirty years later, I feel it is appropriate to share some incidents that have been kept from the public view and how the relationships that grew from these incidents affected my personal development. Because I am human also and have plenty of ego, I'll probably always wonder if our relationship affected Bill's development in any way. No, I shouldn't take credit for that.

CHAPTER 1

—————— ● ——————

An Uncertain Beginning

Up-Canyon View From The Ranch

"That can't possibly be it—it's way too wonderful a setting with the river, the up canyon views of the high country, and the gentle slopes of the pastures," said my wife, Judy, as we looked across the river at the only home visible at the address we had been given, "we'll just have to wait for the agent to show us the way." I parked the truck and turned off the engine. The sound of the river was a gentle murmur overlaid with the raucous calls of flashy black and white woodpeckers flitting from oak tree to power pole and back, the grass on the hills above us was turning green from the gift of moisture since the winter rains had begun, and on that afternoon the sun shone brightly but gently in the December sky. As we soaked up the ambiance the real estate agent drove up, waved merrily, and said, "Follow me!" driving right to that perfect place. The other vehicle following her also pulled in and parked, and as the occupants piled out she began introductions with "This is William Shatner; you may recognize him as Captain Kirk on Star Trek." When we regained our composure, we said, "Nice to meet you!" and really meant it. Suddenly we understood why the agent had been so elusive about giving any more information than "There is a new owner who may want a caretaker for the property they have just purchased if you are interested." We now wondered, "Wow, are we really going to get a chance to live in this little piece of paradise?" Looking back, it's interesting to me that we really were more excited about the prospect of living at that beautiful property than we were about possibly being associated with a celebrity.

Three Rivers, in the foothills of California's grand Sierra Nevada Mountains, is a place of special beauty, and has an aura of love and peace of heart. In 1978 this unique community gained the attention of William Shatner and his wife, Marcy Lafferty. They were looking for a country home for a retreat from busy schedules, and fell in love with the leisurely pace of these hills. Three Rivers is the only place along the Sierras where there is a clear up-close view of the high country, where the above-timberline crags are easily visible without being blocked by the foothills. The forks of the Kaweah River, after which the community is named (Main Fork, South Fork, North Fork), flow all year and provide wonderful views, swimming, fishing, floating, and soft or torrential sounds, depending on the rains or the snowmelt in the high country above, and provide the water that is stored in Lake Kaweah below Three Rivers for power generation and summer irrigation in the fertile valley just down the canyon.

The word "Kaweah" is from the Yokuts tribes of Indians that frequented the canyons, higher up in the heat of the summer and lower down the rivers where the winters are mild when the high country was snow-covered. There seems to be some magic in the word as well as the area and the way it affects those who spend time on or near the river's tributaries—it grabs hearts and minds, and attaches great, strong strings that draw people back to Three Rivers from wherever they wander. Whether in the constant movement of the water, the inertia of massive granite boulders that line the canyon walls and floors, or in the bedrock mortar grinding locations of the ancient dwellers, the effect is the same on all who are susceptible to those feelings.

My wife, Judy, was raised in Orange County, in the then small town of Placentia, but her maternal grandfather had homesteaded a 640-acre section of land on the South Fork of the Kaweah in 1908, and she was blessed to spend most of her summers on the ranch he developed, riding his horses in the summer sun and then playing in the river to cool off. Her father had an orange grove (Orange County was named for those groves; there was a time when they really were there) and after irrigating would bring the family to Three Rivers for a few weeks until the next watering was due. Grandfather Lovering, known as Whispering Bob in spite of (or because of) his bellowing voice, split off an acre on the river a half-mile downstream from the ranch house, and when Judy's father sold the orange grove and retired, they moved there. It was a wonderful time and place to be a young girl, and those strings that pull many of us back to Three Rivers were deeply embedded in her soul. I learned of this wonderful place much later, in the early 70's, but almost immediately fell in love with its grandeur, its scenic beauty, and its good people, but most of all with the warm, embracing spirit of Three Rivers.

Bill and Marcy also were affected by this spirit, and made an offer on an eighteen-acre ranch on the South Fork, a couple of miles upstream from Judy's grandfather's place, and overlooking one of the swimming holes Judy's family frequented. The Shatners' offer was accepted, and in January, 1979, they excitedly took possession of their new ranch.

Judy and I had determined we were going to move to Three Rivers from where we had been living in Idaho, mostly to be near some of her family members as they grew older, but also because we loved (and still do love) living in that beautiful, comfortable area. The South Fork, especially, holds a magic that settles our souls.

We arranged for Randy Stoor, one of our real estate licensees and the most knowledgeable in the building business, to take over management of the Idaho office and continue the real estate and construction activities there, and we brought our travel trailer and parked it at Judy's mother's place on the South Fork. I planned to commute to keep my hand in the Idaho business as long as needed, expecting to spend time there every month until Randy could buy us out. Sounded good at the time, but as Warren Edwards, an old ranch foreman on a summer job I had during high school would tell me, "Always keep your mind fixed so you can change it." As I relate the upcoming events, you will understand why I am glad I remember that advice.

We owned some properties in Three Rivers, but vacant lots only, so had been looking for a place to rent until we decided where to locate permanently. Judy talked with the real estate broker mentioned earlier, Gladys Lukehart, about finding a rental, but Gladys was very evasive. It wasn't long before she called us and said we needed to talk. We met at her office, and again she was vague about details, saying only that there were people from Los Angeles who had purchased a property on the South Fork and were looking for someone to live there and care take the ranch since they would only be coming to Three Rivers occasionally. She gave us an address and said she and the new owners would meet us there that Saturday if we were interested. We talked it over and decided to at least meet with them.

Our arrival at the ranch, as told earlier, was momentous, as the ranch arguably is the most beautiful location on the South Fork, with mostly gentle slopes, a generous water right, an old barn, and a nice enough house, all bordering the river just upstream from one of Judy's favorite childhood play places, where she swam and slid downstream on the smooth river rocks. The fences and pastures showed some years of little or no maintenance, but the site was wonderful. It is in a wide spot in the canyon, where another canyon comes in from the south. The modern ranch house is perched on top of a gentle ridge, with pastures all around and wonderful up canyon views of Mount Dennison and South Fork Ridge. Judy and I could hardly contain our enthusiasm about having a chance to live in that spot, even if only as a rental. When we were welcomed to the place and introduced to William Shatner, he was accompanied by his wife, Marcy Lafferty, and his business manager, Victor Meschures. After a brief tour of the grounds, we went in the house to discuss possible business and occupancy arrangements.

Now the real question came to our minds: How much rent would they want for this wonderful place? Victor, the business manager, said they expected to provide the home to live in, in exchange for duties to be defined, caretaking the property and being paid separately for work outside the scope of a caretaker. Judy and I instantly liked that, and told him we'd like to go on with the discussion.

Victor said one of their goals was to make this a working ranch, and could we raise some cattle or something to make that work? We discussed irrigation, fences, and the rejuvenation of the necessary things to accomplish that, and Victor asked how many cows we could raise on the 18 acres. Since none of us had significant knowledge of how much irrigation water was available, I suggested that four or five would probably be a prudent number to begin with. Victor looked really disappointed, and said, "I was hoping maybe 40 or 50. How do you raise cows, anyway?" I reviewed briefly the life cycle of raising cattle for market, finishing with "and when the steers get to maybe a thousand pounds, they are ready for slaughter." Victor immediately asked, "Why don't we keep them until they are thousands of pounds?" then paused a moment as I looked at him speechless, and said, "Oh, I guess they don't grow that way, do they?" I knew immediately we had some educating to do at the business office.

While I was justifying how many cows could be raised on that small acreage, Judy interrupted with, "Why don't we raise horses instead of cows, they smell better!" Bill, who had been mostly listening, jumped into the conversation with "Oh, let's do that, I like horses much better than cows!"

7

That settled it. The decisions were: (1) Judy and I would live at, care take, and manage the ranch, (2) I would start shopping immediately for horses, (3) the horse ranching business would be an informal partnership/profit sharing arrangement rather than an employer/ employee relationship, and (4) all the other details like irrigation, fences and other improvements we would work out over time. We happily moved into the house to begin our experience of hobnobbing with (and educating) the rich and famous.

Probably Judy and I considered this a major victory, to know we simple country folk had garnered the trust of these people who lived in that Hollywood world of peddled influence. And especially, we were very cautious not to take advantage of that trust in any negative way, but would do our best to develop the ranch as if we owned it ourselves, giving it our very best efforts.

In the early stages of the relationship Judy and I had developed, we determined it would be more important to live where we wanted than to be forced to live where we could earn a living. The decision to move in to the ranch fit right in with this predetermined philosophy, and we were totally comfortable with it at the time.

●

CHAPTER 2

Naming the Ranch

Ranch Sign at Entry

Bill and Marcy wanted to have a suitable name for the ranch, and much discussion spread over many hours of an early visit produced nothing that felt good to them. It had to be the right name. Everybody had suggestions, but none seemed to fit.

Toward the end of the day Bill came excitedly to the ranch house and said, "We've got it—Marcy has named the place 'Belle Reve' which is French for 'beautiful dream.'" We agreed that it certainly suited the whole concept of why the ranch was acquired, and how it was expected to be used. It really suited Judy and I, for that was exactly what we were doing, living our dream of spending some of our life in Three Rivers, specifically on the South Fork. Being associated with a celebrity was just an unexpected, interesting bonus for us.

Some 110 years earlier than the arrival of the Shatners at the ranch, the year 1867 had an exceptionally wet, early winter. The ground was beyond saturated—it was soggy and heavy with water. About eight or nine miles upstream from the ranch, according to accounts found at the Three Rivers Historical Society, on the south side of the river a massive chunk of the mountain that forms South Fork Ridge gave in to the extreme weight of water held by the soil and plummeted down the steep canyon wall, bringing with it part of the forest and about one-third of the grove of Sequoia trees now known as Garfield Grove. It came with such force that it carried a massive volume of huge trees, boulders, and more soil than most people thought existed in that rocky terrain, totally blocking the canyon to a great depth. The result was an instant, temporary dam across the canyon, and a reservoir of dirty, angry water began to build behind it.

The only South Fork homesteader at the time, Joseph Palmer, later telling of this remarkable incident recalled that it had been raining in the foothills almost steadily for 41 days and nights, and on the morning of December 20 it began to rain in the higher elevations, saturating the already heavy snowpack. "Just before midnight," he states, "I was aroused by a heavy rumbling sound such as I had never heard before, and which lasted for an hour or more. Then a great calm set in, and even the roaring of the river ceased." It was nearly three days later that the loosely formed dam broke and with a mighty roar a wall of water and debris rumbled down the canyon, the flooding reaching more than forty miles out into the valley to Visalia and beyond.

Fortunately, there were no human casualties, as the South Fork had only the one resident. As the tumbling torrent passed what became Shatner's ranch, the river changed from its usual gentle flow to a raging torrent almost a half mile wide, scraping out a new riverbed, exposing huge bedrock slabs, and changing forever the channel of the Kaweah. It carried its burden of huge granite boulders and trees, including giant sequoias, rapidly down the canyon. The sequoias are very brittle, and as they were thrown against the huge rocks in the enlarged riverbed they broke into many pieces which were left scattered down the canyon and even out in the valley as the flash flood waters receded. Over the ensuing years the locals salvaged some of those redwood chunks and milled them into slabs.

Back to 1979: Judy's sister, Teri Ohlwein, a really good graphic artist by trade, and her husband, Leuder, a remarkably skilled wood worker and carver, were living at Grandfather Lovering's original homestead, just two miles down the South Fork. Leuder had in his possession a redwood slab cut from wood believed to have been left by the 1867 flood, roughly three feet by four feet, four inches thick, and the ownership commissioned Teri and Leuder to design and carve a sign that expressed the feelings the ranch fostered in Bill and Marcy. The final design retained the natural, irregular outline of the slab and held the carved heads of a mare and foal in a pose of loving closeness, and in a classic style the name "Belle Reve Ranch." It was perfect. Bill and Marcy loved it, and we placed it at the entrance to the ranch. It is still there, and now that it has aged, is even more attractive.

To complete the look of the ranch insignia, Teri designed, and with Leuder's help built, a stained glass panel of the head of a horse to be installed in the front door, a door Leuder made from a solid redwood slab, probably also part of the Sequoias that came down the canyon in that great flood some hundred years earlier. Everything about the ranch was filled with the spirit of Three Rivers.

CHAPTER 3

●

Horse Business Goals

Dalan, Judy, Marcy & Bill (on Dandy)

Raising horses is a long-term thing, both in terms of the life of horses as compared to other crops and in establishing a name and reputation in the business. There are many levels of participation or ownership, from recreational riding to complete breeding operations. None of us felt capable of managing a full-fledged breeding operation, complete with one or more stallions and a band of broodmares, nor did the ranch lend itself to that, especially with the hilly terrain, remote location, and lack of needed structures; nor was Bill's business manager anxious to make the required investments, since Bill was currently in a tight financial situation. We learned that an actor's life is as uncertain

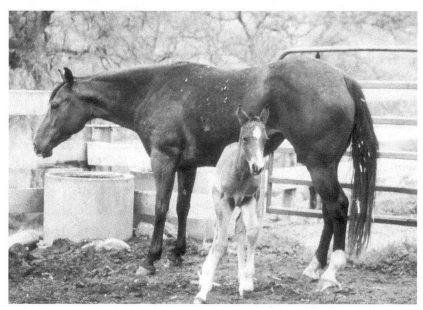

Broodmare & Baby

at times as any of us who choose to be self-employed, perhaps even more so, because being employed depends on the opinions, efforts, and whims of agents, casting people, writers, producers, directors—one of the many reasons I didn't envy Bill his occupation. As to the horse business at the ranch, we decided a more logical operation was to own some good quality broodmares and breed them to outside stallions, raising the babies for sale.

"What kind of horses do you prefer?" I asked Bill. He said, "I don't know, what do you prefer?" I told him my preference was quarter horses, specifically of cow-horse blood lines, as sometimes the racing lines were high-strung and hard to handle, and my personality just gets along better with those that are more laid back. Also, to keep the investments in a reasonable range, we would not acquire "top of the line" horses, but those with good breeding and still offering potential. Bill agreed that would fit in with the general feeling of the "Beautiful Dream" ranch he was creating, and said to go ahead and find some better-than-average mares to begin building a broodmare band.

Since we had just come from Idaho, and since I was still commuting there often, I consulted with a horse rancher friend in Bern, Idaho by the name of Dean Kunz. He invited me to visit him in Rexburg where he taught some equine classes at Ricks College (now BYU-Idaho) and had a stallion that was a son of Doc Bar. Doc Bar was the buzzword name in the horse business at that time as he and his sons, horses with names like Doc O'Lena, Dry Doc, Doc's Lynx, Doc's Oak, Doc's Remedy, and others, were top performers or producing top performers, especially in the cutting and reining horse worlds. We determined to focus where we could on Doc Bar bloodlines on one side, and began to look for foundation or super performing cow horse lines to cross them on. The most promise of great performance seemed to come from Doc Bar lines crossed with mares descended from Poco Bueno, another great older sire, especially through the Poco Tivio lines. One of the factors that we felt affected this performance seemed to be that the Doc Bar horses brought the speed and fire of his sire, Three Bars, a leading running horse sire, into the cow horse lines, complimenting the slower, gentler nature of the cow horse without diluting too much those instincts that make a cow horse a cow horse. Other sires that showed real promise were the King Ranch horses (the San Peppy lines) or the Freckles horses.

The horse business is often quite serendipitous. It soon came to our attention that a man named Bud Gooden, living in Exeter, less than thirty miles from the ranch, had some foundation bred mares that were close up to the great foundation stallion, King, through Rocky Knox by Rocksprings. Mares of this type of foundation breeding were also a really promising cross on the Doc Bar sires, as the cow horse instincts so essential in a cutting or reining performance horse were protected, even enhanced, so we went to look at his horses and with Bill's approval wound up buying two or three immediately, and more later. These mares became the core of our broodmare program.

It is essential that the cow horse instincts be preserved and actuated in training, for these instincts are what make the difference in a performance with a cow, whether in cutting, reining work, or working a cow on a ranch for gathering, branding, doctoring, or moving to another location. The horse with these instincts can anticipate the cow's next move and place the horse and rider where they need to be to control the situation, much as a bird dog, or retriever, uses its instincts to hunt or retrieve. The trainer of the animal merely sharpens these instincts and embeds in the animal's behavior the proper way of thinking about each situation. As training progresses and these autonomic actions grow, the instinctive moves go well beyond what the trainer taught into a realm of actions guided not by thinking, but more by reflex, increasing the speed and effectiveness of each move.

The effects of these genetic traits are very real, and breeding horses to preserve and enhance their abilities is an essential key to successful cow horse breeding. Just as horses bred to run seem to want to do that above all else, cow horses want to work a cow above all else. These were the traits we were looking for in abundance as we shopped for mares and selected sires to take our mares to.

CHAPTER 4

•

A Personality

Bill Riding Dandy in Ranch Arena

As we got to know Bill, we found him to be a lot of fun, entertaining to be around, and one who is passionate about everything he does. He is really personable, seems willing to get along with about anybody, and is always trying to make sure he is communicating. We could all learn from that.

Although early in our relationship he was somewhat strained financially from the uncertainty of an actor's life (apparently also there was a problem with a former business associate and finances), he didn't let that keep him from developing the ranch, even though we were constantly aware of the cost of all we did. It was important to him to build it right, and he was committed enough to do so. That was no problem to us, as we were used to working businesses within budgetary constraints. Also, he was in between film projects, and income remained limited for a time. It was a little later that he was in demand again. This was to us an indicator of his character, that he was willing to keep looking up and thinking positively in a time of pretty dire straits. Those of us who have struggled at times probably appreciate that more than those who have had it relatively easy in life. Most importantly, he continued to enjoy visits to the ranch and spoke appreciatively of the progress it was making. Bill was constantly was aware of our feelings, and tried very hard to make sure we were satisfied with the progress being made, which was pleasing to me to know that the early trust placed in us was being upheld.

It was interesting to see him separate his personal, ranch life from his very public professional life. The ranch was a private, family place, where the public was not invited. It is situated near the end of a private lane, which is off a little-used, dead end (except for a non-public fire and ranch access) road off the South Fork, which was also a dead-end (and then more than now) little-used road. There he seemed to feel safe from the prying eyes of the paparazzi or the curiosity seekers, and was able to relax and be himself.

It was that "self" that I found hard to define. Much later I realized that he had been an actor for so long, and had become so used to putting himself into a role described in detail in writing and verbally by those creating and directing the action, that he seemed most comfortable when being instructed in that same degree of detail, no matter what he was doing. Apparently his confidence level increased with instruction. Opposed to this was my own upbringing of having little direction, instruction, or conversation about many of the actions of life, figuring out things on my own, learning by watching, and being perplexed by others' inability to see what needed to be done, and then do it, without verbalizing each action first. I was not very comfortable doing the directing, since I did admire his celebrity status, yet found that was often quite necessary as we spent time touring the facility or discussing the horse operation. Judy aptly describes his state as a "blind innocence" about things needing doing on the ranch.

Over thirty years after these first experiences I read Bill's book, Up Till Now: The Autobiography, and gained some insights into how his mind works. Perhaps that characteristic which was most evident in all he did, and also very evident in his autobiography, was the speed at which his mind travels. He can ask questions and be off to the next ones before most people can formulate an answer to the first two or three. Judy and I marveled at his ability to search the depths of any action, again apparently as a result of needing to put himself into a character and operate as that character operates. Although in his autobiography he claims that the best directors he worked under were those that "left me alone," it became evident to us that his position of so capably operating or portraying a character would only come into play after he fully understood from screenwriters and directors what was required of the character and the situation being played.

Bill's love for his family was foremost in all he did. His girls spent as much time at the ranch as they could, and he made sure they learned to enjoy it like he did, especially Leslie, the oldest of the three. She seemed to fit into the Three Rivers mentality more than the others, and passed this characteristic on to the family she and her husband, Gordon Walker, produced somewhat later. It was important to her, as it was to Bill, that the ranch was as self-sufficient as possible so if some calamity made the city unlivable they as a family could be safe at the ranch.

While at the ranch Bill kept pretty much to himself and his family, unless there was a business matter to be discussed. We respected that privacy, and didn't ever invite people over to see the celebrity, but kept his visits quiet. The location of the ranch was not advertised or made public. In fact, this writing, in respect for his privacy, was not even considered until after the ranch had a public visit day in April, 2011 as part of the "Hidden Gardens of Three Rivers" tour to benefit the Three Rivers School. That tour was, thanks in large part to the draw created by his name, a success beyond anything the organizers had dreamed, and they are grateful for his cooperation in allowing his private place to be featured. At the close of that tour, and partly because of the inconvenient location, Belle Reve became again a very private place.

Apparently over the years the location of the ranch has become common knowledge to some, as a few days ago I was talking with some out-of-state visitors who were kayaking on the South Fork and they referred to one of their river entry places as "the Shatner point" as they would put into the river from the bridge leading to the ranch. I didn't say anything to them about having a connection with that "point."

There are two things about Bill and our acquaintance with him that I think exemplify his personality, the first being his energy, his zest for everything he does, and his abandon in enjoying simple things like a dip in the river, or a hike across the pastures, or the way he is captivated by a newborn foal. He is a remarkably complex person, but has the ability to commit himself completely to what he is enjoying at the moment, no matter how simple it may seem. We could all learn from that. The second thing would be that he genuinely cares for his family, his friends and all that are dear to him. He is lively, but kind; he values his privacy, but loves to share himself and his talents with those close to him. I was always treated as a friend, and have a great respect for that side of Bill.

CHAPTER 5

—————— ● ——————

Idaho Flashback

In order to build the ranch to what we all wanted it to be, I found huge demands on my energies, both physical and mental. Besides the time needed to work with and direct those hired to help build irrigation, fencing, etc., I needed to still spend daily telephone time keeping the Idaho businesses going, and yet the proper development of the ranch demanded more and more. It is my personal philosophy that no development should be done, especially in an area as spiritually sensitive as Three Rivers, without spending enough time there to find out what non-physical needs will be serviced by the proposed development and honoring the demands of those needs in any proposed changes. There are more considerations than those addressed by zoning laws or land-use planning regulations, and those intangible yet very real considerations require massive amounts of time and mental energy to reconcile them with proposed changes, even when the changes are simply from one ranch use to a different ranch use. These times of thinking and pondering over what was needed were not considered to be hours of "billable" time that I could charge the business office for, yet they were necessary, in my way of thinking, to get it right, to produce the proper long-term benefits to Bill and his investment as well as maximizing the enjoyment of our family as we lived, worked, and played there daily.

So the reader can understand what demands were in play as we built the new ranch, it is important to note that Judy and I were not wealthy, but still had debt from building the Idaho business, debt that we planned to pay off with proceeds from the sale of the Idaho business, our Idaho properties, and if needed some of our Three Rivers holdings. The ranch was providing us a place to live, rent free, and some income from building projects, but our less-than-perfectly-thought-out arrangement did not always provide sufficient income to meet our daily living needs. Well, we thought, we'll make it work until some proceeds come in from the horse business. In the meantime, the Idaho office will produce some income, and it was doing that, though not ample. We were still so infatuated with the idea of living in this wonderful place that we remained blind to the inherent financial hazards of the seemingly great life we had fallen into.

We were encouraged when before long we had an offer on our Idaho house. The buyer seemed okay, but financing was really hard to get at that time, so we determined to finance it for him on a wrap-around contract, quite common in that period. We took a very small down payment, and the buyer's payment would pay our existing loan and give a little extra to us. The monthly income would help cure our cash-flow problem, and it would get the buyer in the house to take care of maintenance, critical in the winter in Idaho. We quickly closed escrow.

The Idaho office, meanwhile, under Randy's direction, seemed to be doing okay also. I arranged to visit often, and had an opportunity to acquire from a friend on really easy terms a Porsche 924 for the trips to Idaho and back, which made the nearly 2,000 mile round trip much more fun. It really helped to be familiar with some of the back roads of Nevada, southern Idaho and northern Utah, as I used these relatively deserted stretches to eat up many miles at speeds that I should be ashamed of. After a few trips I found Randy's capabilities diminished the need to be there as much or as long as before, which was a relief. We were really pleased with ourselves and our new life in Three Rivers. It seemed that all would be well, after all.

CHAPTER 6

•

Building a Brood Mare Band

Broodmare "Buddy" and New Baby

With our basic band of mares, we began shopping for stallions to breed these mares to, preferably of the popular Doc Bar breeding. Here we ran into a problem with Bill and the business office's budgeting. Those most popular stallions (those that were siring performance winners) were quite pricey in their stud fees, so we had to lower our expectations a notch and breed to some local stallions, including Broadway Doc, located in Fresno. He was an own son of Doc Bar, and out of a mare called Fancy Three, by Three Bars, so the potential was there, but he had not sired any real high-earning cutting performers yet. One of the problems of the business even today is that the best trainers tend to promote certain lines of horses, creating more winners in those lines, and not having enough time and energy to branch out into other lines with potential. How many of these well-bred horses would become high earners if given the chance by a top trainer and enough campaigning? We didn't know if the owner of Broadway Doc had the wherewithal or the inclination to campaign him or some of his offspring to prove him as a sire, but would have to take that chance.

To broaden our base of talent, and therefore our opportunity to sell more young horses, we wanted to breed to some proven stallions in reining or snaffle bit competition, as well as in cutting. We succeeded in getting the business office to okay breeding one mare to Mr Gunsmoke, a producer of winners in the snaffle bit and reining as well as in cutting competition. This great producing sire is Leo-bred, bringing good speed into the cutting horse lines. His fee was relatively high for the time, as I remember, $5,000.00. This was a princely sum for our little operation, but we felt it really desirable establishing the name and reputation in the business that we wanted to. This required taking a mare to Temecula, California, and got us acquainted with Gary Wexler, who was standing Mr Gunsmoke there at the time. This acquaintance proved to be very beneficial for the next three or four years while Gary was maintaining a high profile in the cow horse business, and became our entry into a circle that let us breed mares to other winning horses like Montana Doc (a full brother to the famed Doc O'Lena), who was being campaigned heavily by Gene and Margie Suiter, and winning both in the Open and Non-Pro cutting shows. The Suiters were at that time moving their base of operation from Arizona to California. Montana Doc was consistently winning in the Non-Pro Cuttings with Margie riding, and then Gene would ride him in the Open, very often winning both classes. It was quite some time later that the Doc O'Lena horses, of which Montana Doc, a full brother, was one of the early winners, became so well-known as winners and producers of winners.

Other leading stallions we took mares to included Doc Tom Tucker, who was standing in Redding, California. The amount of travel we did to get mares bred will seem foreign to those in the horse business under today's rules. The rules then were that a mare had to be on the premises with the stallion, including when artificial insemination was used, as a breeding was accepted for registration by the AQHA only when the mare was on the same premises as the stallion. It required a lot more transport of horses then than it does now. Judy and I had traded our travel trailer for a motor home and used it to tow the ranch horse trailer and mares to many destinations.

Sometimes we weren't able to get a booking with a syndicated or otherwise restricted stallion, so we shopped for young horses that were the offspring of these stallions. This led to the ranch purchasing a filly by the great sire Dry Doc, another full brother to Doc O'Lena. This filly was a stocky little sorrel with a big white blaze, and seemingly endless athletic ability. We kept her until she turned two and was ready for training, then sold her as a futurity prospect. We eagerly kept track of her progress, but apparently an unknown physical problem kept her from completing training and she went into service as a broodmare.

After a few years in the business we saw the market changing, with the "mid-grade" horses we had been building our business with becoming less and less in demand, and only the top lines that were consistently winning maintaining their value in the sales. This pushed us to try to move up, and we cautiously increased the budget numbers as we shopped for new mares.

CHAPTER 7

● ───

Fencing Pastures

As we acquired horses, we examined the old fences. They were seriously in need of not only repair, but rebuilding, and the decision was made to do three-rail wooden fences built of 2x6 boards for strength. Judy's first comment was, "Whatever else we do, let's not paint them white, because white fences always look like they need new paint." She was right, as usual, and we decided the fences should be black, as that blended in to the landscape and didn't need painting as often. Also, anti-chew or other coatings an active herd of horses may need in the future are most often black, so that would fit. Bill and Marcy concurred that practical is often the most desirable, certainly being swayed by Judy's thoughts about the expense and inconvenience of keeping white fences white.

The layout of pastures, as stated earlier, was done to accommodate access to the barn from all points, and to give a variety of pen sizes. One of the rules of being really successful in developing a ranch or other property is to not rush the job. Taking some time to get to know the property, to feel of its spirit and blend with the natural flow of the land and recognize its demands is what brings success that lasts. As we planned and laid out fence lines, Bill was mostly absent, so we had pretty much free rein to set it up in the manner our experience and feelings dictated. The years since have proven the effectiveness of the layout, as it has proved to be very functional.

We shopped for posts and lumber, and found a supplier who would deliver. Building board fences is a difficult job for one person, so I hired help—Judy's son, Scott Kraemer, who was off on his own, worked with us for a while, along with a friend, Rudy Thomas, from Oklahoma. They pitched a tent down by the river and became temporary residents as they built fences, and became so comfortable there that they invited guests, who thoroughly enjoyed also. It was in this period that our first granddaughter, Kassie Kraemer Ward, was conceived, with whom Judy established a relationship immediately after her birth, and has filled her life with love ever since.

An early, welcome discovery in the fence building was that the ranch has soil, as opposed to the rock so prevalent in most of Three Rivers. A rented power posthole digger would allow us to put up most of the fences quickly. When Scott and Rudy moved on, Bill sent up from Los Angeles a worker named Alazar.

One day Alazar and I were building a fence in the Grouse Creek bottoms, when Alazar shouted to get my attention. I was crossing the creek on a log and stopped to see what he needed. His English was no better than my non-existent Spanish, but almost instantly he communicated, with a wagging finger and a buzzing of his lips, pointing to the creek bed below my feet, that there was a rattlesnake. I moved on across the log, then got off to look where he was pointing, and sure enough, there was a rattlesnake coiled in the shade of the log I was crossing on. Because of the danger to our valuable horses we eliminated the snake, and Alazar concurred that was the proper thing to do. Language barriers can be overcome if there is a need, I decided.

The first summer we found the ranch had an abundance of rattlesnakes, probably because it had been largely unused for a few years, and they had free rein of the pastures. We killed several, all large and healthy, and hoped the population would dwindle after that, which it did. I especially remember one large snake, probably three and one-half feet long, which isn't big by Western Diamondback status, but it was extremely thick in the body, and looked really strong. A snake of this build seems to know how powerful it is and carries itself accordingly, broadcasting an awesome aura.

I had just come out of the barn and started toward the house, carrying a pellet gun I used for pest control on ground squirrels. The snake was moving down the side of the road and stopped when I came into its view. I thought, "I've never tried to kill a snake, especially one this big, with a pellet gun," and aimed at its head. When I pulled the trigger, I was disappointed to see the snake's lower jaw drop as if it had come unhinged, as apparently I had hit it too low, not in the brain as I had hoped. The snake turned and headed for the barn, crawling through the still-open door. I didn't want to lose sight of it and not know where in the barn it was, so I followed. As it crawled under the manger seeking safety, I saw Judy coming down the hill and asked her to bring a real gun, with which I dispatched that slithering safety hazard.

The largest rattlesnake I have personal knowledge of was killed by Judy's brother-in-law, Leuder, on the back lawn of their home just down the South Fork from the ranch. It measured eighty-two inches long, just two inches short of seven feet! One of the locals skinned it, dried the hide, mounted it on a board, and hung it on the wall of a local hangout, The Indian. I have wondered what happened to that decoration when the establishment closed, but I have no desire to own it, so have not asked.

Painting the newly-built fences was a real chore. Nobody seemed to want that job, and as I asked neighbors who may be available, Manuel Andrade, a local stone mason and friend, volunteered his daughter and son. They painted diligently for days, were good workers, and dependable. Recently I asked Christine Andrade Burns, the daughter, if she remembered the job, and she said she would never forget it. She doesn't remember now why she and her brother, Tim Andrade, were so "in Dutch" with her father that he would give them that really unpleasant work assignment, but she is sure it was something serious he was getting even with them for.

CHAPTER 8

•

Horse Sales

Dandy in the Pasture

Auctions are an amazing event. The frenzy of bidding for a popular horse is so exciting as the ring men shout bids to the auctioneer, waving their hats to get his attention and encouraging bidders to become buyers. On the other hand, when there are few or no bidders on an animal it is really depressing to see no response to the cries of the auctioneer as he tries to generate interest, dropping his starting price lower and lower. We sold, and bought, several horses at auctions, and each was an adventure. I still get feelings of anxiety in my stomach as I think of the strain of trying to get horses sold (or bought) within the price guidelines we had established.

Offsetting this strain is the camaraderie of the horse people we met and looked forward to seeing at subsequent events. I remember one sale at the Snaffle Bit Futurity in Reno that was especially long, going until close to midnight and still many horses to sell. We were spectators only that year, and enjoyed visiting with Jerry and Nancy Rapp and their son, Phillip, who later became a leading cutting horse trainer and rider. As the sale wore on, none of us really wanted to stay any longer, and suddenly Jerry said, "Let's go bowling!" I asked, "What did you say?"

Jerry explained that the MGM Grand Hotel and Casino, at which they were staying, had a wonderful bowling alley in the basement, and we should go bowling. We left the sale and spent until the wee hours of the morning bowling and visiting, thoroughly enjoying being away from the strain of the sale.

The highlight of the west coast sales was the Wexler sale, where we were expected to wear black tie and tails, fancy boots, and act like we were the upper crust. It worked for some, and some of the others of us just enjoyed the food and atmosphere. The food was exquisite. It was there that I discovered "turkey nuts", deep fried turkey testicles. I thought I would founder, I so enjoyed them.

One spring we took some young horses to a sale in Sacramento and thought while we were there we would buy a gelding for use around the ranch, if we could get one that seemed suitable, and at a reasonable price. Usually Judy and I went to the sales, but this time Bill said, "I'd like to go with you and bid on a horse, an auction looks like it would be fun," so he came along.

There were some of the usual complications of a celebrity being in the party, but most quarter horse people pretty much keep to themselves and allow those around them to do so, as well. A few recognized him and asked for autographs, and Bill was pleasant about giving them. Jerry and Nancy Rapp were there along with their son, Phillip, who was about twelve years old at the time. He was a good conversationalist, even though still young, and Bill really enjoyed visiting with him.

In order to be as visible as possible (an asset as we established the ranch in the business) we had positioned ourselves on the front row of the sale, right in front of the auctioneer, Duane Pettibone. He also had become a friend, and we were comfortable dealing with him. We had gone through the sale catalog with Bill before the sale and marked those geldings we may want to bid on, then previewed each one. We knew pretty much which horses would be best for our purposes and how much we would be willing to pay for each of them.

As the sale proceeded, we bid on two or three, but the prices went higher than our predetermined limits. Bill was enjoying bidding, and followed our business plan very well. He did a good job bidding on one of the horses we were interested in and was the high bidder, buying a nice gelding at a really good price, but the auctioneer, Duane, motioned he needed to see me outside. He explained that the horse was meant to have a reserve price higher than we had bid, but the owner's agent that was to bid it up had somehow missed making a bid, and the horse wasn't really to be sold at our bid price. In asking us to give up the purchase, he let us know that we could hold him to the sale if we needed to, but would like to have us not buy the horse. I agreed, told Bill we didn't get the horse, and we went on with the sale.

It wasn't long before a really nice four or five-year old gelding named Dandy Doc Tucker came in the ring, a beautiful bay with a petite head, big hip, short back, and trained well enough for our ranch purposes. We had allowed a budget price of $1,600.00, and the bidding passed that, so we dropped out. I went out to refresh my memory on the next one we had on the list. As I inspected that prospect, I half-listened to the auction going on, and in the background, I heard the auctioneer announce that Dandy had sold for $2,600.00. Not thirty seconds later Bill appeared, looking really frantic, and excitedly said, "I just bought that horse, what do I do?" Then he told me what had happened. He was visiting with Phillip, having one of their animated conversations, smiling and nodding at Phillip, when he turned away from Phillip and looked up at the auctioneer, still smiling and nodding, and of course the auctioneer took that as a very clear buying signal, slammed down his gavel, pointed at Bill, and said, "Sold!" Bill panicked and hurried out to find me.

I simply replied to his question of what to do about the horse he had purchased by mistake, "Pay for it!"

Yes, I realized that the auctioneer owed me a favor and we could have cancelled the sale, but it wouldn't have been good for our business reputation, Bill being as visible as he was, and besides, it was a really good experience for Bill. The bonus was that Dandy turned out to be a real joy of a horse, both for us as a ranch horse, and for Bill when he later took him to Los Angeles for riding there. It was almost thirty years later that Dandy was allowed to retire and spend his last days in the lush pastures of Belle Reve Ranch in Three Rivers.

CHAPTER 9

—————— • ——————

Personal Growth

T he new-found confidence from successes in building the ranch fostered feelings of being more in control of my own life, and I determined to start a supplemental business that would allow us to remain at the ranch as long as we desired. Because my real estate experience in Idaho had been generally positive, we started looking into what was required to get similar licensing in California, and found that affiliation with a broker for a period of time was a requirement. I had not felt a desire to be associated with any of the existing offices or brokers we had met, so I hadn't determined what to do in that regard.

One day as we drove up the South Fork toward the ranch, I saw the shape of what appeared to be a real estate sign nearly covered by grass and fallen leaves under a big oak tree, back a ways off the road. Out of curiosity I stopped, climbed over the fence, picked it up, wiped the dead oak leaves off, and sure enough it was a real estate sign, "Marty Wolf, Broker" and had a phone number. It was really curious to us that neither Judy nor I had heard that name before, so when we got home I called the number. Sure enough, Marty Wolf answered, and our conversation led to a meeting. His age had caused him to scale down his activities in his advancing years, but he still enjoyed the thought of being active in the business.

Marty was a long-time resident of Three Rivers, had owned Lake Elowin Resort for many years, and knew most of the people in town.

His reputation was good, and he and his wife, Dee, were exceptionally personable and easy to get to know. Everyone we talked to about them seemed to like them and we received no negative reports, so I felt this may be an opportunity for both of us to benefit from an association.

He was thrilled to think that I had the capability and was willing to manage his office and build it up again, and he could work if he wanted to. This would give him a lift, and would serve my purposes in gaining the California licensed experience needed for a broker's license. We struck up a working arrangement, I took and passed the sales licensing test and began promoting my name as a real estate agent in Three Rivers. Because of Marty's good reputation, we had business almost immediately, and I was greatly encouraged. Maybe this would be the way to earn at least a modest living while at the ranch, and it would keep me actively involved in real estate while our Idaho properties were still for sale.

CHAPTER 10

●

Bill Meets Our Family

Kristi, Bill, Carolyn, Terry, ca. 1980

Our kids were initially a little in awe to think they were going to be associated with a real celebrity, but probably not for a reason Bill will want to read about. Judy reminds me that the first thing Kristi and Terry asked him was, "Do you know Barry Manilow?" I've wondered how his ego reacted to that. Besides getting that most important question out of the way, all of us recognized his star status. The Star Trek series was still current enough to be well remembered, and Bill will always be a hero to those who enjoy watching those entertaining, even if sometimes simplistic, shows, as I still do.

As I was writing this many years later, I e-mailed my children and some other family members for their reaction at the time to us being associated with this celebrity. The answers from extended family members were pretty universally ho-hum, that it was no big deal. Judy's girls that lived with us, Kristi and Terry, were quite fascinated to meet and spend time getting to know him. My kids, Carolyn and Chris, lived in Nevada and, though they spent time with us at the ranch in the summers, both met him but didn't get much time with Bill. It's interesting to hear the things each of them remembers the most.

Chris took a message to Bill at his house at the ranch one hot summer day for me, and he remembers that Bill answered the door in his underwear. It apparently hadn't occurred to Chris that Bill was a human, but that brought reality to him, to know that Captain Kirk can be casual when out of uniform. Bill and Chris really enjoyed their association, and I'll write in another chapter about Bill's gift to Chris when we left the ranch some years later. Chris had admired my Porsche when he was still too young to drive, but a few years later he showed up for the summer with one of his own, a 914, and I don't know where he learned to drive fast, but he could really negotiate the South Fork with that car. It's good there was not much traffic in those days.

Carolyn writes that she was initially excited to meet someone that was on television, but that thought evolved into a feeling of appreciating his talent and ability, and that just being in the limelight doesn't make anyone more important than someone else of great ability. She shares a family trait of wondering why that limelight on others so affects those of the "fan club" mindset.

Terry apparently felt his mind moved too fast for her comfort. She did recall realizing that when he asked "How are you?" he wasn't really looking for an answer, but just being sociable, not expecting a response, and his mind had already moved on to something else. Asking a youngster to comprehend anything other than a direct answer seems to be somewhat of a stretch, and it didn't sit well with Terry to be asked to make that adjustment in her thinking. Perhaps she was jealous, or at least envious, that someone else's mind may move faster than hers.

Kristi loved watching the Star Trek reruns, so she was really excited at the idea of meeting Bill. However, after a few of his visits when she was the one elected to catch the horses and get them ready for Bill and his family to ride, including brushing and saddling, she began to feel like "his little worker" and some of the magic disappeared. "He became just another person to me, not the star I had seen on TV," she notes. She also is enough of a rider to notice right away that their riding style of "posting" like an English rider did not really mesh with the western tack and horses we provided for them.

Judy is the movie follower of the family, so she knew more about Bill than any of us, and had enjoyed his acting talents. She really looked forward to meeting him, and when she did her feelings of his energy and enthusiasm were borne out.

Judy and I had become close to our nearest neighbor, Hat Maxon, and considered him almost as family. He was older than dirt, it seemed to us, had enjoyed Three Rivers all his life, and was full of personality. Hat loved to sing an Indian song about "Little Redwing" to anyone who would listen, and we sometimes took Bill to Hat's to be entertained.

My own feelings about Bill were much like those of Carolyn, centered around the basic premise that everyone, even celebrities, perhaps especially celebrities, gained the respect of those around them by actions more than reputation. As I got to know Bill, he became a friend, and I valued that.

Because Bill didn't get to spend much time at the ranch, the kids (or any of us, for that matter) didn't get much time with him. I'm sure he had enough admirers in his daily life that it felt good to just get some quiet time, some alone time. We were happy to let him have his privacy, as we valued our own.

CHAPTER 11

●

Kosher, or Not?

Victor, Business Manager, ca. 1979

Awhile after we had moved to the ranch, Bill and Victor notified us they were coming for a visit. Judy volunteered to make brunch if they arrived before lunchtime, which they did.

One of the finger foods we enjoy is rumaki, made by wrapping in bacon a chicken liver and a water chestnut, covering with butter and brown sugar, sticking a toothpick through to hold it together, and broiling until the bacon is crispy. Yum! It had not crossed Judy's mind, or mine, that a majority of successful Hollywood business managers are of Jewish extraction, and have certain taboos in their diet, one of the highest priority ones being anything to do with a pig. Bill, Vic, and I were in the family room discussing ranch plans and progress when Judy proudly brought in a sizzling tray of rumaki, and the aroma filled the air. Victor asked what it was, and Judy told how these morsels were made.

When Victor declined to take some, Judy was disappointed, then it suddenly dawned on both of us the faux pas of offering to serve a pork product to a member of the House of Israel. Oops! Judy was embarrassed beyond words. She felt so bad, but recovered nicely by serving the other (and acceptably kosher) things she had prepared. Vic felt bad too, to embarrass her, but stuck to his principles.

As a member of the Church of Jesus Christ of Latter-day Saints (Mormon) I have a deep regard and respect for those of Jewish descent, the most well-known surviving branch of the original House of Israel. Through that lineage of Judah came Jesus Christ, the object of our devotions and to whom we owe our deep-seated beliefs, even to the point of LDS members of Gentile origin claiming membership in the House of Israel, by adoption, and accordingly espousing many of the same beliefs and principles as the ancients. Our common heritage goes back to Abraham, Isaac, and Jacob. Mormons have experienced persecution in similar ways to the Jews and have kindred doctrines and beliefs such as a mutual belief in Jehovah, a God of revelation; a belief in the Messiah who shall come; reciprocal beliefs in prophets; and a common commitment to the return of the Jews to the "land of Jerusalem" in fulfillment of the words of the ancient prophets.
David Ben-Gurion said to Ezra Taft Benson, a leader of the LDS faith, in a visit to Israel in 1964, "You know, there are no people in this world who understand the Jews like the Mormons."

In October, 2011, Senator Joseph Lieberman (I-Conn) addressed a forum at Brigham Young University in which he said, in part, "I do feel a special connection to the Mormon faith...because of the core principles...rooted in the tradition in the Mormon faith...People of faith share a lot."

Sometime later than the incident above I realized that Victor was aware of the feelings LDS members have of being part of Israel, for one day as we were visiting some religious topics came up, and to show that he understood where my feelings were he said, "Dalan is the only one I know who thinks I am a Gentile!" We shared a good laugh of mutual understanding and went on with ranch business. The rest of the day went well, and bit by bit, our lives meshed as we learned more about these new friends.

CHAPTER 12

•

Grouse Valley

Upper Grouse Valley

Just upstream from the ranch is the access gate to the Grouse Valley fire control road. When we were at the ranch the gate was not secured and monitored as closely as it has been lately, and we were able to travel it often. A little later we developed a trail for horses and ATVs from the back side of the ranch to the Grouse Road that gave us virtually unlimited access, and the owners whose property the road crossed seemed happy to have some neighbors travel the road for security reasons, so we rode it as often as we could.

This road climbs steadily for a few miles until it drops over the rim into Lower Grouse Valley, which has gentle slopes, seasonal waterways, a pond, scattered oak trees and a few groves of evergreens, mostly cedars. This is a wonderfully private, secluded area with a couple of little-used cabins and good road access for those with the right keys and permission. Often we saw bears, coyotes, deer, and many kinds of birds, especially quail (but never a grouse).

About four or five miles above the rim of Lower Grouse is another climb to the rim of Upper Grouse, which at that time was privately owned land, and very scenic. This area also had some rudimentary cabins, two nice sized lakes with fishing, and many pine and fir forested areas. Not long ago the USFS bought this parcel and added it to the Sierra National Forest that joins the area. By then the cabins had been rebuilt, mostly of high quality log construction, and the plan is to have them available for vacation rentals for forest recreation. The access to this new playground is from the Springville side of the mountain, not along the Grouse Road that we traveled.

Only those who love being in the outdoors can understand the magnificence of this kind of country. It is quiet, little used, and those you (once in a great while) meet up with are mostly of a like mind, just wanting to be left alone to enjoy their own kind of solitude. Wildflowers of many kinds abound beyond description in the spring and summer, my personal favorites being the profusion in general and as individual blossoms, probably, depending on which part of the season it is, Chinese Houses and Farewell to Spring.

Winter is an especially lovely time, as an occasional snow and frequent rains keep the soil moist to show fresh tracks of deer and bears. It is so great to find a bear track left in the fresh snow as he wanders around looking for breakfast, and the deer are easier to see when the grass is white.

It was just below Lower Grouse Valley that Chris had his first quail hunt. One of his summer visits stretched into fall, and knowing that I had hunted a lot when I was young, he wanted to try it. As we moved up the road I got a chance to bag a quail, but Chris, so far, had been out of position to take a shot. My bird dog, Rufus, had been trained to hunt when we lived in Idaho, and was really excited to have us trudge through the woods as he scurried around following his nose, as bird dogs love to do.

41

Before long it became desirable to split up to cover more territory, and just after Chris and Rufus headed around the other side of a grove of large oak trees I heard a gun go off, then Chris' voice, full of excitement, shouted "Get it Rufus, fetch!" I looked that direction just in time to see Rufus on a dead run, weaving through the oaks, chasing a quail Chris had knocked down, grabbing it skillfully and then reversing direction to proudly carry the prize to Chris. As I grinned, almost laughing out loud with the happiness that the success of my hunting partners brought, Chris shouted, "Dad, I got one!" The day was a complete success.

CHAPTER 13

———————— • ————————

Idaho Business Update

It's a rude awakening to the holder of a note to not receive payments as agreed. This was suddenly the case on the Idaho house we had sold and financed. The buyer was out of work, and now had moved out of the house, expecting us to take it back. Of course, we did take it back to protect our equity position, but now we had to clean it up and sell it again, in the meanwhile making the payments on the underlying mortgage. Real estate was in a slump, as interest rates in the early 80's had gone really high, and Randy had no immediate prospects for a sale of the house.

Because of the slump, the office was not producing much, either, so our cash flow position quickly became quite critical. Construction projects on the ranch, those that paid, didn't pay enough to much more than get us by, but we appreciated having those. I piloted the Porsche to Idaho again, put the house back on the market, held a cheerleading session for Randy and the business, and went forward.

It may have been on that trip that I learned one of the hazards of driving a Porsche. I was traveling through Nevada on a two-lane road in the middle of a group of three or four other vehicles all exceeding the speed limit by fifteen miles an hour or so, when a highway patrol car showed up in the opposing traffic lane, apparently with his radar operating. As we all zipped past him I was relieved to know that I was not alone in this infraction and should therefore be safe. Wrong. I saw

43

in the mirror that he flipped his lights on, made a U-turn, screamed past the two vehicles behind me and pulled in next to my rear bumper motioning at me to pull over. When I asked him why he pulled me over out of the middle of the pack he said, "You were going over the speed limit." Right away I got the idea that it wouldn't do any good to protest. A while later, as I pulled into a small town somewhere in Nevada one of the others who had been in the "pack" recognized my car and came over to sympathize. He chuckled as he expressed that he didn't understand why I was the one chosen to get the invitation to contribute to the State of Nevada.

It wasn't long before Randy had another offer on the house, but again we would have to finance it for the buyer, again with minimal down. "Well," we said, "maybe this time it will work," and we negotiated an acceptable price and terms. Randy was happy to earn a commission, as the high interest rates had virtually shut off the real estate business. An example of how out of reason interest rates in general were was pointed out to me when I went to an escrow company with financial documents for a transaction I was handling in my California business. I was working as a buyer agent for a wealthy investor, and as the title officer scanned the financial statements involved her eyes got big, and she looked at me in amazement, saying, "I've never known anyone who had a million dollars in their money market account, and do you realize he's earning about sixteen percent on that now?" The point is that rates were really high, and financing was too expensive to buy a house except in really unusual circumstances, so Randy was working a lot but not getting far. I began to worry about the feasibility of him buying the Idaho business from us, but since there was nothing I could do about rates, I just returned to the ranch and enjoyed Three Rivers and the continued satisfaction I received from building the ranch as we waited for the Idaho uncertainties to work out.

In the meantime, the trips back and forth from California to Idaho provided some relief from the stress of these uncertainties, and gave me hours of think time to work out solutions to things going on both in Idaho and at the ranch. Now and then, a little excitement occurred on the trip, also. I remember one time I was traveling across the deserted roads north of the Great Salt Lake in the early evening hours. The sun had just gone down and the jackrabbits were coming out to feed. The road has long stretches with no curves and I was enjoying having the road to myself as I crossed the wide open spaces at speeds that were exciting. I was able to see far ahead, and I could see a small spot in the road in the distance. As I approached, I honked the horn, but the spot didn't move. By the time I realized it was a rabbit, I was too close to safely swerve to miss it, and glanced down at the speedometer as I heard the "thump" on the bumper. I had slowed down to ninety-five miles an hour. No doubt the poor rabbit didn't feel anything, but it still was not a desirable thing to have happen. As I drove toward Nevada and California I couldn't keep from having thoughts relating the untimely demise of an innocent rabbit to the sudden death of the Idaho business. I admit that not all of my "ponder time" as I drove was pleasant and uplifting, but it was still a pleasant trip.

CHAPTER 14

●

Borrowed Underwear

O ne of the things Bill wanted to do in the first summer after we got acquainted was tour the ranch, now that Judy and I had been there long enough to be really familiar with the environs. We walked fence lines and ranch boundaries, looked at the South Fork river, which was still quite swollen with icy cold runoff from the high country, then crossed over the ridge below the ranch house and went down to the edge of Grouse Creek near the southern boundary of the property. It was so beautiful, the grass turning to its golden hue of summer, wild flowers still blooming in spots, trees fully leafed out now, and Grouse Creek, which springs up in lower elevations and warming in the sun, murmuring gently through the rocks, truly an ideal environment. Bill was so enthralled, so thrilled to think he owned a part of this beauty.

We sat on the grassy bank and visited a while, then Bill got up and took off his shoes. He walked into the stream, feeling the cool water on his feet and ankles. He stepped out on the bank, and looking around as if to wonder if anyone else was nearby, he stripped to his shorts and jumped into the deepest pool of the creek. He lay down in the water and it hardly covered his body, the stream was so small, but he loved it, splashing and laughing like a youngster, really enjoying the abandon of a new, rich experience.

Bill got out of the water and let the sun dry him off, and as we walked back to the ranch house Judy asked if he would like to borrow some underwear for the trip home. I guess that is the closest I got to being a celebrity, when a pair of my shorts went to live in Hollywood.

CHAPTER 15

Adding to the Acreage

The original eighteen acres was adequate for the size of the horse operation we were establishing, but not long after the initial acquisition another thirty or so acres adjoining the upstream side of the ranch, the only parcel between the ranch and the Kenwood property, became available unexpectedly. It just made sense to acquire it, as not only was the price right, but also it had some additional pastures, mostly free of rocks and gently sloping, as opposed to much of Three Rivers being rocky and steep, and most importantly, a good water right on the same ditch we were already using. By this time I had completed my state-required period of licensing with Marty Wolf, and had obtained my broker's license. Soon after, I established my real estate office and named it, with Marcy's permission, Belle Reve Realty. Through this office I handled most of the negotiations for the purchase of the property and suddenly the ranch more than doubled in size. We established good, strong fences and access roads and the extra pastures were easy to add to the irrigation system.

It seemed to me to be a real coup to acquire this, as good irrigated pasture is so scarce in Three Rivers. Bill and Victor didn't, I don't think, ever realize how fortunate they were to get that property. To the business office it was just another transaction, but the extra acreage became really useful in later years when Bill expanded the numbers of horses at the ranch, and gave options for potential growth.

CHAPTER 16

— • —

Planning the Irrigation System

T he irrigation ditch that feeds into the sprinkler system is the original ditch engineered and dug in the early 20th century. It heads in the South Fork stream about half a mile above the earliest use of the water, and is really a scenic trip. The ditch has wild ferns and cedar trees along its banks and to walk the route seems as wild and private as any wilderness area. Garry Kenwood, who had the first ranch to use the water, was in charge of keeping the trail open and passable, and each year I would help him with the pruning and trail renovation. There is a huge growth of blackberry bushes that seems to want to eliminate the trail each year unless the stems are cut back to allow access, and the ditch itself needs cleaning and patching of the banks after the winter rains.

Visiting with Garry as we worked on the ditch was a treat. He had been an animal trainer for the movies for years, and had just recently returned to Three Rivers to live in his boyhood home with his aging parents, Frank and Muriel Kenwood. Garry's list of accomplishments was long, one of the last being training/handling of wolves for the movie, Never Cry Wolf. He had an amazing knowledge of animals and communicated with them in a remarkable manner. It's another example of the diversity and talents of Three Rivers people and the blessing of how they share with those around them.

The key to successful livestock farming is always water, whether for irrigation or drinking. In these semi-arid Sierra foothills there is seldom any rain from June to October, and pastures dry up, providing little or no feed if not irrigated. The importance of water and the right to use it cannot be overemphasized, and I stressed this repeatedly to Bill and Victor. Their experience in this area seemed less than I had hoped, and it was left to me to determine what needed to be done to protect the water rights and establish the infrastructure for the use of those rights.

I used Garry as the main research source for the ditch, as he had grown up with it and understood its use better than anyone. We discussed how much water was available, and if it would be there all summer. The answers were that there was a generous water right, plenty of water for the acreage, but the soil didn't lend itself to running water through a ditch for any distance, as it just soaked into the ground and disappeared. Having been raised on a farm in Idaho, I knew exactly how that worked, and also what the remedy was. We had piped water to many fields on hillsides below canals, using the pipes to keep the water moving rather than letting it soak into the ground. Also, the natural slope of the hills let gravity provide the power for sprinklers for crops or pastures.

The San Joaquin Valley, just twenty miles downstream from the ranch, is the highest producing agricultural area in the nation. It also relies heavily on irrigation, and I thought a phone call would get some real help in setting up a system. A representative from an irrigation company showed up almost immediately, and we began with a tour of the ranch and where the water was coming from. As we discussed how many pastures we would water, he asked, "Where do you plan to put the pumps?"

I said, "We don't use pumps, we're going to let gravity pressure the system."

49

We went on with our tour and discussion, and pretty soon he asked, "Where are we going to put the pumps?" I shook my head and reiterated, "We're not using any pumps," then continued the discussion.

It wasn't long before he asked, "Where are we going to put the pumps?"

I may have been raised in the country, but I feel I have some knowledge of human potential, and decided his qualifications were minimal when it came to gravity-flow irrigation systems, so I thanked him for coming all the way up to the ranch, and sent him back to his flat valley environment where he could sell pumps.

I figured the other companies from the valley were probably of a similar mindset, so I went to town and purchased a surveyor's level and other things I needed to do the layout of the system myself and began the planning process.

CHAPTER 17

———————————— • ————————————

Building the Irrigation System

Sprinkler in Operation

The ditch that brings water to the pastures is over a hundred years old, and well established although needing constant maintenance. It always has a good flow, even in low-water years. Also, it comes onto the ranch property near the base of a steep hillside some distance above most of the pasture land, a perfect situation for a gravity-flow system.

Most important to this type of system is "fall", the vertical distance from the beginning of the system to any sprinkler or other outlet. Water builds pressure at the rate of one pound of pressure for every 2.31 feet of vertical fall, so by measuring elevations it is easy to see where sprinklers will be effective. With the help of our newly-purchased surveyor's level, I ran some grades and found my hunch was right—there was sufficient fall for a good system.

I went to the most knowledgeable, experienced construction firm in Three Rivers at that time, Britten Construction, and asked the owner, Larry Britten, to come to the ranch and review what I wanted to accomplish. He had experience with a lot of projects, and felt this one would work well, so I hired him to do the tractor work. His backhoe operator, Bobby Jensen, went to work, I bought pipe and headgates, and in short order we had a pond built where the ditch comes onto the property, and inlet pipes and an overflow structure to fit my specifications. The easiest part was routing the line down the hill to the pastures, as I could check grades as fast as Bobby could dig the trench for the pipes. There was an amazing lack of interference from rocks compared to most Three Rivers projects, and we were really pleased to make good progress. The pipe was laid, connections made, and the system was ready in a few days for sprinkler connections.

Selling Bill and the business office on a "big gun" system, sprinklers with large nozzles that cover a diameter of a couple hundred feet, was reasonably easy. This is an efficient way to irrigate a pasture, and reduces not just the installation cost but also maintenance and repairs over time. Besides, these are really impressive to watch as they rotate slowly, spraying a stream of water high into the air, and because of the gravity-flow system, with no expense for energy to create the pressure. When we first turned on the water, I just stood there and watched for a long time as the water we had captured in the new pipelines wet the parched earth as the nozzle turned, the oscillator not making the "foosh-foosh" sound we are used to hearing from ordinary sized sprinkler heads, but going "FOOSH----FOOSH", and the cooling stream of clear water falling on the thirsty grass all around.

A check of water flow and pressure proved the viability of the system. There was enough pressure to sprinkle efficiently nearly to the top fence line of the original acreage, increasing as the hill sloped downward toward Grouse Creek, and at the lower pasture the "no pumps" system generated about ninety pounds of pressure. We included a small extension of the line to supply the only other user on the end of the ditch, our neighbor "Hat" Maxon, giving him a really useable water system for the first time in years.

Getting to know the neighbors was a treat, especially "Hat" Maxon. His name was actually Harrison Darwin Maxon, and he had lived on the South Fork for double the number of years that I had been alive. I never was able to find anyone who knew where the name "Hat" came from, but that is how everyone knew him.

Hat loved visitors, and our family took advantage of that to listen to his stories about the Indians who lived here before us, and to hear him sing the song "Little Redwing" (I think it was) about lost love before the white man came. Themes seem to be universal in the music world, and everlasting.

As Hat grew older Frank Root and his family came to live with and care for him, and Frank still enjoys telling of taking Hat for rides up the South Fork and having Hat point out with his cane the rocks that still had visible hieroglyphics from the earlier inhabitants, and to listen to stories of the real frontier days of Three Rivers, including when a mountain lion jumped on the back of a mule, expecting to make it lunch. According to Hat's story, the mule thought otherwise, bucked the lion off, kicked it so hard it couldn't get up, then jumped backward and continued kicking until it killed the lion.

It is an emotional experience to create something as successful as the new water system was in bringing life-giving moisture to the soil and a feeling of revitalization to the human spirit. We could now see the grass being green all year, the animals always having water to drink, and the cooling, refreshing spray from sprinklers doing their job. The success of this project boosted my confidence considerably, and seemed to bring me, at least in my mind, to a more comfortable state of being as we settled into the growth and progress of the ranch.

CHAPTER 18

●

Ranch Layout

B ill thought it would be nice to have a pond in the main pasture, especially since we had virtually free water to flow through it and keep it fresh. I spent many days walking, standing, sitting, just spending time on the ranch, deciding what would be the optimum layout to accomplish our goals of providing pasture for horses without destroying, and perhaps even adding to, the views that were so fantastic. Bill's next visit gave me a chance to get his ideas on locating a pond in the main pasture between the ranch house and Bill's house. This would be visually pleasing, and since the slopes limited the size, would not take away too much pasture. He agreed, and we scheduled Britten Construction to do the excavation. It proved to be the perfect location, once again validating my feelings that the planning process is often more time-consuming than the building, but is where the energy needs to be put for optimizing the result.

The location of pasture fencing just came naturally with the terrain, and as we split pastures into new, sprinkler-irrigated sections we provided lanes to move animals from one pasture to another, with all these travelways coming together at the main barn. Then we added some shelters in the pastures where horses could get out of the rain in the winter and find relief from the heat of the summer sun.

Roads were already established, and we didn't want to move these, but the main entry road into the ranch did need one realignment. There was a kink in the road where it crossed a ravine that was too sharp a curve for longer vehicles. One day when a rancher was delivering a horse we had purchased, he realized the wheelbase on his trailer was too long and was not going to make the corner. Since the problem was on the lower side where there were no fences he just sped up and when the trailer wheels dropped over the edge he was going fast enough that they came back on the road on the other side of the curve. I called Britten Construction again and we rerouted the road to form a more gentle curve, the bonus being that this gave us room for another, small pond on the upper side of the road. I have wondered what the business office would have done about the liability exposures we eliminated by this change, but instead of emphasizing this aspect of ranch layout I put most of the emphasis on the visual and aesthetic side. Just as well that Victor didn't get his blood pressure up over what may have been.

Now and then we still get asked if it snows in Three Rivers, as the trip to the ranch seems long, the road is winding, and it is definitely uphill. The actual elevation gain is about 1,000 feet in the six miles up the South Fork from downtown Three Rivers, but it is a big change in weather in the winter. Yes, the ranch got snow a few times while we were there.

The most memorable storm came in the night, when a gentle rain turned quietly to heavy, wet snow and in the morning I was greeted with a winter wonderland of white on all the pastures and the trees; the shrubbery was smashed and the fences and posts were capped, a sight really unusual there. Judy was late waking up (that means anytime after daylight) and I suspected the winter weather would be a surprise, even though we had just moved from Idaho, where she had seen plenty of snow. As she rolled over and opened her eyes, I opened the drapes in the bedroom.

She looked up, gasped, and, as she later told it, thought for a moment, "How did he get me back to Idaho?" Then she realized it was the ranch, it was snow, and it would now be snowman and other play time, which we made the best of, knowing this unique show wouldn't last more than a few hours at the most.

Included in the planning for ranch layout were really domestic things, like where to build a house for Bill and Marcy, where to put a household orchard, which areas could be improved to provide better pastures, and other considerations that would affect the long-term livability of the ranch. These and all the decisions regarding how the ranch would be designed were worked out one by one over a relatively long period of time, again to assure that the feeling of security and centeredness of this lovely place was protected.

CHAPTER 19

—————— • ——————

PCQHA Article

The March, 1982 issue of Quarter Horse Of The Pacific Coast, published an interview with Bill by Jill Scoponich, Editor. I am including, with the permission of the Pacific Coast Quarter Horse Association, this article in its entirety as Appendix A, and Jill's editorial comments on the interview in this chapter. I think her editorial gives a good look at how Bill affected people, as told by someone outside our immediate circle of influence, and the interview (Appendix A) fills in some factual things about the owner/manager relationship at Belle Reve Ranch.

AD INFINITUM

(Editorial by Jill Scopinich, The Quarter Horse of the Pacific Coast, March, 1982)

It's hard to interview an actor. Especially if you happen to be a fan of his or hers. You see him on the screen and know that what you're watching is not really a person but a piece of celluloid—an image, carefully groomed, characterized, conceived by masters of the art of fantasy to be exactly what he should.

If you like the image, you become a fan. You follow the actor through various roles. You get to know him, in a way. You read about him—meet his wife, children, animals through articles in magazines. You form a one-sided kinship with him and become authoritarian when you talk about him with others. (He is too six feet tall! I read it in a magazine! I know all about him!) It's as though he's a member of your own family.

But what happens when the image suddenly becomes real? When he walks up to you, shakes your hand, and you realize this idol of yours is actually human?

I can't speak for everyone, but let me tell you what happened to me (I should say us, the magazine staff) when I interviewed William Shatner for the article which appears in this issue.

I had met Mr. Shatner very briefly at Gary Wexler's sale last August. It was such a surprise and happened so quickly I hadn't had time to get nervous.

Following our short conversation, which centered on his interest in cutting horses and Belle Reve Ranch, the idea of approaching him to do an in-depth interview for the magazine developed. Through his ranch partner, Dalan Smith, I made contact and the date was set for Saturday, November 14 when he would be in Sacramento for the Pacific Coast Cutting Futurity Sale. The interview was to take place in the PCQHA offices.

Now I, like most folks, consider myself somewhat sophisticated. Through my job I have met and spoken with many prominent people and have usually managed to present myself in a courteous, intelligent manner. (Except when I was introduced to former football star Walt Garrison and, trying to sound knowledgeable, I asked him if he had played for the Houston Astros. He very kindly set me straight when he replied, in his slow, southern drawl, "No, ma'am. You see, they play baseball and I played football.")

So the prospect of interviewing Mr. Shatner, most noted for his role in the hit television series Star Trek, shouldn't have phased me a bit. But it did.

You see, I'm a Trekkie—one of those died-in-the-wool Star Trek fans who has seen every episode at least three times. Captain Kirk (Mr. Shatner's role) is my favorite character.

As the big day approached, I realized the magazine staff would be working that day. I also knew how the sudden appearance of William Shatner sauntering into our office would affect them. Naturally, I wanted us to appear casual about his visit—as if people of his stature strolled in and out of our lives every day. So I decided it would be wise to tell them of the interview ahead of time. Besides, I knew I'd have heck to pay if I didn't warn them.

On Friday I calmly made the announcement. I also cautioned them to not mention it to anyone. (I was afraid of having 23 people just 'happen' to stop by the office on a Saturday, all with five friends and relatives in tow.)

Too late, I saw one of our favorite advertisers rounding the corner, asking what it was they weren't supposed to tell. We were stuck, so we added one more to our 'right to know' list and told her about the visit. "Oh, wow! My son is a real fan of his. I think I'll just happen to drop by the office tomorrow and bring him with me," she said enthusiastically.

Normally when we work weekends the magazine staff, myself included, looks as if we're going to work at a horse stable rather than a horse magazine. Jeans, sweatshirts, no makeup, hair tied back or straight is the usual uniform. But on the big day, we all could have passed as staff members of Vogue. It's amazing the change one person's presence can make on otherwise normal, intelligent people.

Midway through the day I was congratulating myself for staying so calm and cool about the interview. I was in complete control, everything was ready and the tape recorder had new batteries. I looked at the clock and realized 15 minutes remained until his scheduled arrival. Just enough time to freshen my makeup and comb my hair. I walked into the ladies room, flipped the light on, looked in the mirror and nearly died! While I had managed to remain calm on the outside, my insides apparently weren't behaving as well, for there on the end of my nose was a great, big, gross pimple! Here I was, a woman in my thirties—too old to be going through this ridiculous adolescent prank—with a pimple on my nose! I felt like I was going to my first prom!

I ran from the ladies room, stood in the middle of the magazine office and yelled, "Oh, my gosh! I have an interview with William Shatner in ten minutes and I grew a pimple on my nose! Help!"

Thank heavens for Marna. She had some kind of stuff guaranteed to erase even the most obscene eruption. I grabbed it, returned to the mirror, smeared it on and, wonder of wonders, it worked! I was whole again!

Unfortunately, though, my confidence I had so carefully cultivated the past few days had nearly disappeared. What little that remained left when I walked out just in time to see our advertiser and her son and his girlfriend standing in my office, with Mr. Shatner and Mr. Smith coming through the back door. My worst fears realized, I quickly intercepted the two gentlemen, introduced them to the staff, then took them to my office, where I explained that the advertiser and her brood had just happened to stop by to preview their ad. Mr. Shatner gave me a knowing glance, kindly introduced himself to the group and jockeyed himself into a chair. At the same time the advertiser took the cue and, glaring at me, exited.

With all the commotion, I had regained my composure. It wouldn't have mattered, though, because Mr. Shatner has a knack of putting a person at ease. I found him to be genuine, cordial, unassuming, intelligent and professional. I was always a fan of Mr. Shatner the actor. Now I'm a fan of Mr. Shatner the man. But I will never pretend to know all about him. He is far too complex for that.—Jill Scopinich

CHAPTER 20

●

Building a House for Bill & Marcy

Shatner House, Front View

We hadn't been at the ranch very long when Bill announced that he would like to have a home built to spend time in when they could. We hired a local architect, Gary Cort, to do planning and drawings (I found out later this was his first project in Three Rivers), and while he was doing his preliminary planning we looked for a contractor. It was convenient that I had been in the building business in Idaho so I could oversee the work, but because I wasn't licensed in California I needed a licensed contractor to work with. Our friend Larry Kreutzkampf fit right in—not only was he a licensed builder, but his wife, Kathleen McCleary, consented to help with the decorating. In a much later conversation Kathleen admitted she was not trained as a decorator, but Larry had just thrust her into this position and everyone involved gave her virtually free rein. Because of her background with antiques and valuable furnishings, and a real talent for matching things up, she did a wonderful job. She also confessed much later, a little sheepishly, that in her inexperience as a professional decorator she had neglected to add a markup on furnishings she purchased for the house, but passed them on to Bill and Marcy at cost. They benefited, and I don't know that they ever realized how her tactical error benefited them but not her.

The choice of contractors proved to be fortuitous, as Larry and Bill got along famously. Their egos seemed to mesh like the gears of a fine sports car, and it was a pleasure to see them communicate and agree on what should be done next, as opposed to the way some contractors and their customers get along.

We spent a lot of time choosing a site. Bill wanted to be by the river, but not so close as to be dangerous at times of high water. The final decision was a site overlooking the river, far enough away from the ranch house to respect everyone's privacy, with easy access to the main driveway—great view of the river, high enough above the river to be safe in times of high water, good solid rock to build on, oak trees all around, and the bonus discovered later of Indian bedrock grinding holes just a few yards away, later to be included in his "hidden garden" site. Apparently even the earliest residents on the South Fork liked that location.

Larry was ready to start by the time the architect had plans drawn, so things moved quickly. Permits were obtained, the excavation was easy, preparation for footings fell right into place, then suddenly we realized the bridge to the side of the river the property was on was inadequate; it would not hold a loaded concrete truck.

After some discussion of alternatives (the most important of which was not to let Bill know there was a problem), Larry determined that the answer would be to bring two concrete trucks, one full and one empty. The empty one would drive across the bridge, as empty it was a

Shatner House, River Side

safe weight for the old bridge, then the full one would dump its load into the hopper of a concrete pump with a hose stretched across the bridge to carry the concrete into the formerly empty truck, which, when it was loaded, would go on to pour the footings. The newly emptied truck would then cross the bridge and be ready for the next load coming up the canyon. It worked; the footings and foundation were poured, and the house was under way.

Bill didn't get to see much of the actual construction, as his schedule kept him in Hollywood most of the time, so he missed the joy of seeing the structure grow and the pains of seeing things when they didn't go just right. The only real glitch in construction came when the framing crew couldn't make the floor joist layout fit the dimensions of the plan—and the foundation was already in. It seems the architect had left out the width of a floor joist in his dimensions. A good framing crew is used to this kind of problem, and made it fit anyway.

The house is not large, as that is what Bill and Marcy desired, but is very comfortable and livable. It has great windows and decks to enjoy the views of the river below, and a nice level parking area on the driveway side. Across the driveway is the main horse pasture, with its new pond. Upstream is a wild area (now the hidden garden) and downstream a spot for a family orchard of several kinds of fruit trees. The décor that Kathleen chose for the house was of western styling, in keeping with the horse ranch theme, simple but stylishly elegant, and very comfortable. When complete, it had all the makings of a great family retreat, and has become exactly that over the years. Today, I am told, much of the original decorating is still in use, and is still very much enjoyed.

CHAPTER 21

—— ⦿ ——

Ranch Equipment

The ranch had enough things to do that required equipment work to consider purchasing a tractor. Now, that was a new experience for Bill and the business office. Not in their wildest dreams did they consider how a tractor was used, or for what. For those of us who ranch, it is simply another tool, but apparently not to those with no ranch or farm experience. I gave them recommendations on size and attachments desired, and it didn't mean much to them. Hesitantly, they said I should probably shop around and give them an idea of what the cost would be.

As the saying goes, timing is everything. A plumber in the nearby town of Woodlake was retiring, and had a smaller Ford tractor with a front loader and a backhoe, probably the two tools we would have the most use for, and a couple of other attachments. An inspection showed it to be in reasonable condition, and though small, it would be adequate for ranch needs. The price, when compared to new machinery, was very reasonable. After presenting to the business office the uses we would have for it and the cost, I waited for an answer. The alternative was to hire or rent equipment often, and that logic made it seem okay to them. They agreed to the purchase, I rented a flatbed trailer and went to Woodlake to pick up the tractor. Now the ranch seemed like a real ranch, and when Bill came for his next visit was pleased to see "his" tractor operate, smoothing roads, digging trenches to extend irrigation lines or drainages, and scraping away smaller growths of unwanted brush.

One of the greatest labor-saving inventions for a ranch is the ATV, or all-terrain vehicle. The early ATVs had three wheels, not four like they do now, and were quite hazardous if not operated properly. The ranch acquired and used a Honda "Big Red", the largest and most powerful ranch work horse ATV of the time. It had cargo carriers front and back, large tires, a trailer hitch, and plenty of power. We used it to take fence posts and all sorts of projects from one end of the ranch to the other, and when not working it became a recreational ride up the mountain. The most common use was to get me from one job to another or to check on fences and horses in the far pastures.

One week we had a backhoe hired to finish some ditch work and road building on the upper end of the ranch, and the hill was steep from the pasture up to the top. Carefully I leaned far to the front to put as much weight as possible over the front wheel to safely climb the hill and scooted up to the plateau where the backhoe was. Going back down was easy, but still needed caution to keep from going too fast. No problem, I went to the other project we were working on, and would check on this one again later.

When I came back to do this, I was not careful in shifting down before starting up the hill, and about halfway up lost power, stalled out, and started rolling backwards down the hill. Putting the front brake on just slid the wheel, and I went faster. I knew that stopping the rear wheels could cause the ATV to flip over backwards, but it was either take that chance or crash at high speed when I reached the bottom of the hill. I thought I was putting the brake on gently, but it caught and the front of the machine started up in the air. Too late to get it back down, I had no choice but to ride it out, so as it flipped over I rolled to one side and pushed the falling machine to the other side as it came down toward me. I escaped injury, except to my pride, as the backhoe driver had seen it all. The machine rolled to the bottom of the hill, but had minor damage. Yes, it could have been serious, but wasn't.

There is something about a ranch that seems to take us back to an earlier time of life, part of which included living with the cycles of nature instead of man-made times, and one of the really nostalgic evidences of these cycles is relying on the early-morning crowing of a rooster to begin the day instead of using an alarm clock. We brought some chickens, Banty hens and a couple of roosters, to the ranch and turned them loose to fend for themselves. Nowadays our environmentally-minded folks would call them "free range" chickens, but to us they were a combination of alarm clock, pest control to take care of bugs, and our food storage program. They did provide some eggs in the laying boxes we built, and some we used but most were left for raising more chickens, which gave us a self-sustaining source of good, really tasty meat. Fresh Banty cooked in a cream gravy tastes so much like pheasant that we couldn't tell the difference. We used Banty chickens mainly because they seem better suited to living outdoors by themselves, and also because they are smaller and do not get aggressive like some larger roosters do.

Yes, there is a disadvantage to having chickens in the yard, as they don't seem to be able to learn where fertilizer belongs and where they shouldn't drop their contributions to soil fertility, but this mostly minor inconvenience can be overlooked when the entertainment factor is considered. For example, there is an old-time, wooden hitching rail, made from posts, in front of the ranch house below the canopy of a cork oak tree. We would sit on the front porch in the evenings and watch a procession of chickens come up the hill from the pastures and assemble in a group below the hitching rail. Suddenly one of them would fly up and land on the end of the hitching rail, then move over when another joined it. Pretty soon the rail would be lined with chickens, looking like the digits on a typewritten page, moving over each time the space bar was hit by another body hopping up. When the rail had no more room the first chicken would jump up into the cork oak and find a place to roost, safe from the coyotes or foxes that prowled in the darkness. As this one left, the others would shift over, another would hop up to the rail, the end one would hop up into the oak, and this continued until all were safely ensconced for the night in the foliage of the cork oak tree, and they stayed there until the roosters began crowing the next morning.

CHAPTER 22

◉

Reclaiming the Land

Since most of the acreage of the ranch had been pretty much neglected for a few years, nature had been taking over. Bringing back a civilized setting, other than with the main house, was much like developing a ranch from wilderness. The fences, irrigation ditches and structures, barn, corrals, roads, were all in a state of serious disrepair. The fences and irrigation systems we have talked about already, but some of the real fun was in getting pastures back to a condition that would grow things beneficial to horses.

When Three Rivers was first settled, as with many other places, the early inhabitants liked to surround themselves with familiar things, so plants native to their previous locales came with them. One of these, the domestic blackberry, tended to take over any area that had some water, and promptly crowded out previous plants, including their native, less vigorous, blackberry cousin. The feral vines grew so rapidly and so large and dense that within a few years they were declared by local ranchers to be a pest to be controlled or removed. The ranch had plenty of these when we arrived, covering acres in a couple of locations, and especially along water courses through the place. The pasture areas under these were of no value for grazing, so we began a program to reclaim these pastures.

Bill was treated to some fresh-off-the-vine berries the first summer, and we promised that some berry bushes would be saved for that treat, but most would go to make pastures usable again. The quickest way to eradicate this brush is to cut out or burn the established vines then spray the regrowth, so we hired a bulldozer for the big areas. The operator, Bobby Jensen, had done this many times, and was good at it. He was making short work of piling up brush to burn. I was watching him crawl diagonally down a side hill through berry vines taller than the D-7 dozer, when all at once the blade dropped down the slope and the tractor virtually stood on its blade, with Bobby bracing his feet on the front supports of the roll cage to keep from falling out as he put everything in neutral to see what was going on. The vines were so high and thick that he had been unable to see a ledge of granite several feet high, and had dropped over the edge into the vines below, stopping just in time to keep from tipping over. Luckily the blade had swiveled down the hill and supported everything. Slowly Bobby tried to change the blade position with the hydraulics, and it worked—he was able to ease the dozer off the rock onto the ground below. Once there, he took a much-needed break and we visited a while about the hazards of working without seeing.

After the brush was piled I let it dry and then burned it to dispose of it and get some ground exposed so grass could grow. The county had "burn days" that would allow this, but only when air pollution was in the proper mode. We had to call the local fire station each morning to see if burning was legal. On the day scheduled to burn the piled vines I dutifully called, and the fireman that answered the phone said, "Yes, it's a burn day." I gave him my name and address, then went out to torch off the brush. Regulations were a little easier to live with in those days, and I was able to let the fire run up the hill through some still-standing vines that were old and dry, and it was a spectacular fire. As it burned I looked down at the road that leads to the ranch to see a red pickup truck, a fire captain's truck, coming rapidly toward the pasture. He opened the gate from the road, drove into the pasture and came up to where I was standing. It was Bill Mears, a friend, but also a fire captain. He opened the conversation with, "Do you know it's not a burn day?"

I was shocked, knowing not just that I was burning on a no-burn day, but was on the edge of burn permit instructions by letting the fire run through the vines up the hill as it was doing. How do I explain this to Bill and the business office? I said, "But I called, and the guy said it was a burn day!"

He grinned and said, "I know, my guy 'fessed up;' he told you and a couple of others that it is a burn day, but it really isn't." Then as he watched the smoke rolling up and over the hill, said, "But it should be, the air is moving really well today." I breathed a sigh of relief; I was not in trouble after all.

A few days later Bobby was moving brush at the lower edge of that same pasture when suddenly all forward movement stopped even though the tracks of the bulldozer were still turning. The thing that will do this is water, underground water percolating up through the soil, leaving no structure in the ground to support a machine, essentially creating a quicksand bog. The dozer was resting on its belly, with the tracks clawing fruitlessly at the mush they created as they turned. The hydraulics of modern machinery really give a lot of versatility, and Bobby tried to push the dozer up with the blade in front and the rippers in back, but they just sunk out of sight. We got a chain saw and cut firewood to pile under the blade and the rippers, but it also just sunk out of sight in the mud. Bobby called his employer, Larry Britten, told him of the problem, and Larry came right up. He brought a large front loader and a backhoe. As Larry and I walked to the site, we realized the dozer had sunk until we were taller than the canopy of the roll cage. This was serious sinking. I turned to Larry and said, "Why don't we just leave it there, it makes a great picnic table?" Larry didn't find this funny at all. Maybe he didn't have a lot of confidence that Bill's business office was willing to pay a quarter million dollars for a picnic table.

It took some hours with the backhoe digging holes front and rear, throwing in rock and logs, pushing them down with the hydraulics, doing it again, and again, to get enough base under the tracks so they got some purchase, then hooking the giant loader on and pulling the dozer out. Once it was on solid ground, Bobby stayed far away from that area.

Sometimes, when the berry vines were not too big or the hills too steep, I would clear them out with the ranch tractor. One day I was pushing into a berry patch with the front loader, making good progress, when I saw a really strange thing. The berry vines were coming out of the ground as layers of exposed roots with almost no soil, being peeled off the top of solid granite bedrock, and it occurred to me that there were inverted cones rolling up, so I got off to look. I had uncovered a Native American bedrock grinding site, thirty or so grinding holes, wonderfully preserved, and cleanly uncovered because of the way the berry vine roots peeled off the rock. It was as if the Yokut ladies had just picked up their acorns and gone to fix supper. This was always a special area to me, one I visited and admired many times.

The brush clearing generated more grass-growing areas, and there were a few times when we had excess pastures. During one of these periods a friend needed a place to pasture an aging gelding named Duster, so we brought him to the ranch to graze, putting him with a couple of ranch mares in a small pasture on the east side that had a pond for water and plenty of grass. He was pretty much a "no maintenance" visitor, and a lot of entertainment for the mares as they bullied him around, so we just checked on them occasionally.

One of my habits as I worked around the ranch was to count bodies, as I always knew how many horses would belong in each enclosure. This was an easy way to keep an eye on things, allowing less frequent detailed inspections of conditions of pastures and animals. As I passed the extra pasture one day I noticed that the body count didn't add up, someone was not in evidence. I stopped and watched, considering what horses were in that area, and realized that Duster was not visible. After a few moments of looking, I climbed on the fence for a better view, but still could not see him, so I crossed into that pasture and walked the trail that runs by the pond.

The pond is part of natural runoff from the upper pastures, with a higher dike to slow the flow in one area. When I was crossing this dike I looked down the bank at the pond, and there was Duster in the water, alternately struggling for footing and laying over on his side to rest. He couldn't get enough footing on the steep, muddy bank to climb out, and appeared about worn out, hardly able to hold his head above the water. From the tracks on the dike it was evident that the mares had crowded him off the trail until he slipped down and couldn't get back up out of the deep, slippery mud.

I ran to the ranch house, formulating a rescue plan as I traveled, and got Judy to help. We brought a halter and a long rope. I slid down the bank of the dike and put the halter on Duster, attached the rope, and this was enough encouragement for him to move along the bottom of the dike until he could, with our pulling and urging, get back on dry ground. As he stood dripping water and mud, with his head drooping, looking for all the world like the end of the trail, we changed his name from Duster to "Old Mudder".

CHAPTER 23

◉

Financial Insecurity

Things were going well in the development of the ranch, not as well in the personal life department. The demands of the ranch took first precedence in our life, and often I found that my real estate business suffered from a lack of attention. Over a period of time I tried working out of the office at the ranch, tried opening an office in downtown Three Rivers, then tried affiliating with a Visalia brokerage, but the returns didn't improve much. There were some sales commissions, and there were other rewards.

During the time that I had an office in downtown Three Rivers, I listed a ranch on the South Fork that had limited accessibility because of steep hills and brush. One day I showed it to a potential buyer who seemed qualified and interested, two brothers who were investors, not ranchers, and they had a hard time understanding mostly hidden fence lines and establishing boundaries in their minds. I showed it to them as fully as was feasible without some heavy hiking, then we went to Visalia for lunch at the Vintage Press, their favorite lunch spot.

As we discussed the property over lunch, one of them said, "Why don't we get a helicopter, would that let us see the property?" I assured them it would, but also expressed that I was not willing to pay for a helicopter ride. He reached in his pocket, pulled out a large, heavy roll of $100 bills, and said, "It's worth it to us to see this property, we'll buy if you can arrange it." This was in the days before cell phones, so I excused myself, went to the pay phone in the restaurant foyer, and looked up "Helicopters" in the yellow pages. No listings in the Visalia area, but there was a firm in Fresno that advertised helicopters for rent. I called, yes, they had a pilot in the office at that time, he would meet us at the Visalia airport in an hour.

We met the helicopter, the buyer again flashed his roll of bills to assure the pilot of an ability to pay, and we got in. On the ride toward Three Rivers, one of the buyers kept pointing down and saying, "That property is ours," or "that one belongs to us," and I gathered they did much investing in property.

I directed the pilot to the ranch and we flew the fence lines, getting a good look at the property below, then hovered until the buyers were satisfied they had a good understanding of what it was. As we turned down the canyon to leave, I suggested that since I had ridden to Visalia with them and my car was at my office, it would be sensible to drop me off in Three Rivers. They agreed, and I talked to the pilot, deciding on where to land. There were not a lot of large open spaces available, so as we went up the main fork toward my office I suggested we use the open space of the river to land. We chose a spot just behind the Chevron station (my office was just two doors down), where the pilot set one strut on a large rock at the edge of the river and hovered there as I stepped out on the rock. He took off toward town and I hopped off the rock, climbed the bank of the river to the Chevron driveway and walked with briefcase in hand through some amazed onlookers to my office. It was a great ego trip.

As I was building my real estate business I affiliated with the Visalia Exchangors, a group of brokers who did much work with investors, including exchanges and all sorts of creative financing for problem properties. This was a great educational experience for me to learn these things, and I used many of them later in my real estate career. One of the most interesting was learning to work as a "Buyer Broker" where a broker establishes an agency relationship with a buyer instead of a seller. This works most effectively when the broker is employed by a buyer in a sole agency relationship and does not split any commission that comes from the selling side of a transaction. The ultimate way to work this agency relationship is on a flat-fee basis, that is, to agree with the buyer beforehand what the broker's fee will be to accomplish a purchase rather than the common practice of making it a percentage of the final price. This lets the broker work freely to reduce the price in the buyer's favor, rather than the broker thinking that a reduction in price will benefit his client, but in the back of his mind realizing that the lower price will also reduce the amount of his brokerage fee. Whether or not this will affect the broker's ability to negotiate with the buyer's best interest first will continue to be debated, but the proper use of a buyer agency agreement for a flat fee compensation eliminates this question.

I established a buyer broker agency relationship with a Visalia client, Bob and Karen McDonald, and enjoyed working on some transactions on a flat-fee basis, making some good purchases for him. One day Bob came to me and said, "Karen and I were at the Coast yesterday and fell in love with a property. We want to see if you can buy it for us; if we can get it and some adjoining properties we'd like to develop a new look for that area."

We took a trip to Pismo Beach to see the property in question, an old brick building occupied by a business known as "Toby's Bar". Toby's was just a block off the Pismo pier with a view of the ocean and seemed an ideal location for a nice development.
Bob had some ideas for building a commercial center that would really enhance the main part of the downtown beach area. We determined what my brokerage fee would be to buy Toby's, the key property, and I went to work.

The property was listed with a local Century 21 office, and the listing agent was older, one of those part-time agents that are often not as effective as the more hungry ones, but I wrote an offer on the property and took it to him. A couple of days went by and I received the offer back marked "Rejected." I went to the office, met with the listing agent, and asked, "What was the seller's counter offer?" I was told there was no counter offer. This would not be acceptable to my client, so I asked if the seller was local. "Yes, he is right here in town," the agent replied. I asked, "Can we go meet with him and get a counter offer?" The agent was startled at that request, but called and got permission for us to meet with the seller.

One of the beauties of counseling confidentially and representing a good client on a single agency basis is that not everything has to be shared with another broker, since I am not sharing in any commissions he may be paid, or getting any compensation from the seller's side of the transaction. I knew our offer was low, expected a counter offer, and knew exactly how high my buyer would go to purchase the property. We spent about an hour with the seller discussing his needs and what he would settle for on the property, agreed on a price (which I knew confidentially was well within my buyer's range) and I suggested we write it up then, have the seller sign his acceptance, and if my buyer agreed when I took it to him, we'd have a deal.

We had the paperwork written up and signed by the seller and were getting up to leave when the seller's grown son came in the back door and asked what was going on. His father told him he had agreed to sell Toby's, and the son flew into a rage. He didn't want it sold at all, and certainly not at the agreed-on price. We could do nothing but watch the family disagreement, but the father stuck with his word and told us to take the offer to my buyer and he would take care of the son.

I drove back to Visalia, still shaking my head over the good fortune of timing, got my buyer's signature and submitted it. We were going into escrow on the key parcel of those Bob wanted to acquire. We scheduled for a quick closing, wanting to get that key purchase completed.

There were a total of five parcels we needed to make the development work right, and it was important to us to acquire them as quickly as possible, before one of the present owners got the idea that they could make a killing at the expense of a developer. One of the remaining four was for sale in a family estate. We made an offer, negotiated, and bought the property. Wow, this was too easy, but my client was really encouraged. Two down, three to go.

Another key parcel, on the opposite corner from Toby's, was a small bakery/deli business that had been struggling to stay afloat. The owner was a single lady, a good cook, but seriously undercapitalized when considering the periods of slack business that happen in a resort town. It wasn't long before a notice of foreclosure had been filed on the bakery property. This notice disclosed that the holder of the note was a private party, not an institution, that had financed the purchase for her. We again went to the owner, made another offer to buy her out, not with a large amount of profit, but it would at least get her out of the foreclosure. She turned down our offer, saying she was going to make it work. We waited.

While we were waiting for some progress on the bakery parcel, I approached the ownership of the next plot. This one was owned by a group that was headed up by a real estate broker from Hanford, who had talked some of his clients into buying it as an investment for resale, so we were encouraged that even though it wasn't listed for sale maybe we could get something done on that one while we waited for the bakery parcel to come to some resolution. We determined what the parcel would be worth to my client, then wrote an offer at a figure considerably lower to begin negotiations.

Rather than mail an offer to the broker in charge, I elected to pay him a personal visit. He was mostly retired, just working some deals from his nice home in Hanford, and he welcomed me in. We did the customary small talk, then I presented him with the offer. In a situation like this, nobody shows all their cards up front, so I acted as if the offered figure was all my client would pay, even though it was well under that. He considered the offer briefly, looked over the paperwork to verify the format, smiled, and said, "This is a good offer, we'll take it." I nearly lost my poker face, but held my composure until I had his signature and was back in my car, then grinned and celebrated on behalf of my client. Three down, two to go.

I felt I was gaining weight eating muffins and talking with the bakery lady, but she was holding firm in her resolve not to sell. This made no sense to us, because we had contacted the note holder and found she was not making payments, and the foreclosure was proceeding. We needed that parcel, so we negotiated with the note holder to buy his position in the mortgage note, thus we became the one doing the foreclosure. We let the process run its time, then went to the foreclosure sale to protect our position. Nobody bid at the foreclosure sale, and my client owned the bakery parcel. Four down, one to go.

The remaining parcel was not for sale, period. We could, and were, proceeding without it, but it was space really useful for future parking. Nothing in Pismo has enough parking, and it was important, so we inquired again. Not for sale, nor was it expected to be for sale. We went ahead with our planning on the rest of the project.

It was just a short time later that we read in the local newspaper that the owner of the final parcel we wanted had had a heart attack and passed away. We hesitated to jump in like vultures, wanting to maintain some dignity for the family at that time, but were really interested in what would become of the property. It wasn't long before the probate was scheduled for the estate and the property was included in the list of those to be sold by the probate court. We waited for the sale date, in the meantime determining exactly what the property was worth to the project, and arranging schedules to fit. The sale date arrived, my client arranged funding, and we showed up at the court house in San Luis Obispo for the estate sale auction.

Since I was used to dealing with auctions at horse sales, I was chosen to be the one handling the bidding process in the court room. The beginning bid figure was quite low, and we raised it, along with two other bidders. We raised the bid again and again. The other bidders kept going, then one dropped out. The remaining competitor seemed determined to have the property, but so were we, and the bidding kept going up, a thousand dollars or so at a time. We were within about $10,000 of our predetermined maximum price, and getting worried about how far the remaining rival would go. Now it was time for some horse sale strategy, so I suggested to Bob that we stop raising the price by a thousand or two each bid, but put out our final figure to see if it would blow out the other bidder. Bob was hesitant, but had no better ideas, so he agreed. "Two hundred thirty-two thousand five hundred dollars," I said to the judge, and the courtroom got really quiet. "Going once," intoned the judge, "Going twice." "Sold!" and the property was ours. This was without a doubt the most exciting series of transactions I had ever been a part of, and for it to end a complete success was really a boost to me.

The commercial development that Bob and Karen built is still, almost thirty years later, the most attractive and desirable place in downtown Pismo Beach.

The income from the venture to the beach was welcome, and got Judy and I through quite a few months without real hardship, but the nature of the real estate business is such that when an escrow closes and a commission is paid if there is not another one already in escrow and moving along, there will be a dry spell. To keep up with daily living expenses we sold some building lots in Three Rivers that we had acquired as investments and hoped to keep longer. To reduce outlays, I sold the Porsche I enjoyed so much to eliminate that payment. In spite of these adjustments in our planning, each day Judy seemed happier to be living on the South Fork, and I determined to continue to do whatever it took to keep my family on the ranch, while also recognizing the size of the distraction from my real estate business that it presented. I was content to settle for what the business would produce with that handicap, if it was any way possible.

CHAPTER 24

◉

A Play in Los Angeles

On one of Bill and Marcy's visits, they asked if we were interested in seeing a play in Los Angeles that they were in. Judy remembers it as being Otherwise Engaged, a cute comedy starring Marcy, with Bill as one of the male leads. When we asked if we should bring our girls, Terry and Kristi, Marcy immediately and quite emphatically said, "No!" and Bill agreed, but more quietly.

We let them recommend a place to stay after the show, and the business office made a hotel reservation and arranged show tickets for us. When the time arrived for the trip, we left early to make a day of it, including a stop at the business office.

It was always a treat to go to the business office on La Cienega Boulevard, as the aura there was very professional and we got to feel like we were part of something special. This trip had a surprise, for as we were traveling down Wilshire Boulevard toward the office we stopped at a traffic light, looked at the car next to us, and it was Bill's daughter Melanie. We spoke to her, she recognized us immediately, and we both pulled over for a short visit. What are the chances in Santa Monica of running across one of the very few people we know?

After the visit to the business office we checked in to the hotel, had a nice dinner, and headed for the theatre. Apparently it was the usual Los Angeles theatre crowd, all seeming so sophisticated and in the know, and we really did feel like we were out of our element, as we really were.

As soon as the curtain went up, we were okay again, as the play was very entertaining. We enjoyed knowing two of the leading characters and comparing the roles they played on stage to the personalities we had seen at the ranch. At this time we realized how at home they are in this environment, and what a stretch it must be to try to fit in to the completely different scenarios of the foothills of the Sierras, and this helped us be tolerant of the questionable things we saw in some of their out-of-place visits there, and more forgiving of ourselves when we were in Los Angeles.

Soon we found why Marcy had been so adamant about not inviting the kids to come with us, as she peeled off her blouse for a topless scene. Yes, that would have been a little too much for our sheltered girls, as they were really naïve, at least we as parents thought so. We'll always believe in their innocence.

The next day we were very happy to arrive back at the ranch and fit into the routines and mindsets that suited us so well, leaving the LA atmospheres to those more suited to that.

Probably the closest our girls got to being celebrities was the year Kristi tried out for Woodlake Rodeo Queen. It is a thrill, even if a little scary to her dad, for a daughter to go racing around the rodeo arena in the required maneuvers. She finished as second runner up, and we were proud. Whether she would have scored higher in the judges' eyes on a quarter horse instead of the little Appaloosa we had brought with us from Idaho is only guessing.

Terry was a star on the Woodlake High School diving team, doing well there. She seemed as fearless in front of the group and the judges as she was on the ranch, even though I probably tried to discourage her from trying out for the team. The scariest part of being a parent is when your children start making their own decisions.

CHAPTER 25

◉

Difficult Upgrade

Bill Riding Wicked Witch Fea

The top-of-the-line cutting horses were the Doc O'Lena mares, and breeding to that syndicated stallion was not an option at the time, so Bill and I discussed going to a sale at the Phillips Ranch in Texas to try and buy a mare. When I arrived there, I discovered we needed something we didn't have to be part of that elevated echelon of horse ownership. There were horses available for sale, but those that showed the most promise for training or had the best pedigrees seemed all lined up to be sold to particular buyers, those with the long-standing connections that put them in the "in group" of top horse owners. To break into that circle took a combination of (1) a willingness to spend generally inordinate (at least for our operation) amounts of money for initial purchases and (2) agreements to buy and sell horses, agreements unspoken but well understood, doing business over a long period of time in a manner that helped support the prices of the top horses, thus maintaining the health of that portion of the horse business. I was not in a position to leverage our efforts in a manner that would move us to that level.

I previewed the mares and fillies available at the sale, and discussed with owners the potential of each, then wound up the successful bidder on a two-year old dun daughter of Doc O'Lena. She was bigger than and not as refined as many of the performing cow horses we saw at the sale, but had the pedigree and seemed adequate for our band of brood mares. We were happy to say we now owned an "own daughter" of Doc O'Lena that we could breed to the stallion of our choice. I arranged for the mare to be shipped to the ranch and boarded a plane for home.

One of the greatest cutting horses of all time was Rey Jay, the one-eyed cutting horse. Rey Jay daughters had produced winners, and we ran onto an opportunity to own a daughter that also had been a winner in her own right at several cuttings, named Wicked Witch Fea. The owner wanted a high price, but was also willing to do some trading. We had two fillies that were two-year olds that showed promise, and we traded those and some cash for the mare. She had been bred and came to us in foal, and we eagerly watched for the baby. She was kept in a small pasture below the barn, and a little before her due date, slipped the foal in a stillbirth. We were devastated; we had so looked forward to that baby. Such is the horse business, I guess. At least we still had the mare, and scheduled her to be bred for the next season.

Diversions from this type of incidents were constant, and we relished the occurrences that kept us ever grateful to be in Three

Rivers. We needed some help on a more steady basis for a while, and looked around for someone who needed some work, but not full time. It so happened that our long-time friends Bill and Deni Gillespie were wanting a change of scenery and occupation. Judy had known Bill since high school and had become acquainted with Deni not long after that, when they had babies at about the same time, and Judy and Deni had kept in touch over the years and had become fast friends as they offered support through several changes in life, including living in different areas and each of them marrying different partners and beginning new lives. It was a pleasing surprise to Judy when her new friend Deni married her old friend Bill Gillespie.

Not long after we came to the ranch Deni had expressed to Judy that she and Bill were looking for a new adventure, and we invited them to come to Three Rivers. They came, stayed, and Bill worked at the ranch for a time while looking for other, more permanent employment. He was good help, even if overqualified for most of what I had him do.

Gillespie (I'll call him that to reduce confusion with Bill Shatner) is an intellectual, always playing mind games, and making good comparisons and analogies, and some of them took me quite a while to figure out. He was always content to let things work in your mind until you gave up with frustration and finally begged him to describe what was going on. I remember only one time that I got the best of him.

The east pastures of the ranch (later sold) had some moveable hand lines for sprinklers that we changed early in the mornings, and we would then have time to visit or have breakfast together. I left the west pasture pretty much up to Gillespie to water, with me checking on the condition periodically. I noticed that the grass near the fence didn't seem to be growing as quickly as that further out in the pasture, so when the sprinklers were set in that area I made a point of checking, and found that the water was not quite reaching the fence. There was no reason the water shouldn't overlap into the hill pasture outside the fence, so I wanted to call to Gillespie's attention that he could make his last set closer to the fence. Having friends (or family) work for you is touchy, because correction or instruction can sometimes be taken as criticism, and the last thing I wanted was for him to feel I was not satisfied with his work.

As we were having breakfast together that morning, it occurred to me how I could encourage him to make a change in the sprinkler patterns and still not sound like I was criticizing him. He was buttering some toast and I craned my neck to obviously look very closely at what he was doing. He looked up to see if something was the matter, and I said, "I was just watching to see if you buttered your toast clear to the edge," and went back to my own breakfast.

It wasn't long before Gillespie said, "I know you're trying to tell me something, but I don't see what it is."

"Let it work on you for a while," I replied, and changed the subject of the conversation. Gillespie grinned and nodded his head, loving the game, but he remained very thoughtful for the rest of the meal. I didn't elaborate any more that day, and it is to the credit of our relationship and the power of the intellectual sparring we did that he wouldn't ask again, but all through the day it felt as if the wheels in his head were turning full speed. Still I let it work on him overnight.

The next day he could stand it no longer, and came to work earlier than usual, grinning and shaking his head again. "I don't get it, please tell me what you mean," he begged.

I said, "Let me go with you to change the sprinklers, we'll talk as we work." Instead of letting him move the sprinkler pipes down to the other end, I took the lead and moved them very near the fence, changing his well-established pattern and allowing the water to reach past the edge of the pasture. We had made only a couple of moves when he began to shake his head again, then broke out laughing.

"You really had me going," he said, and we both understood that he was saying he now knew the answer. We explained later to Judy and Deni what the riddle was, and then I confessed it was the only time I had got the best of him. Every now and then Judy and I will still, as we prepare breakfast, ask, "Do you butter your toast all the way to the edge?" and chuckle together at the pleasure of good associations. The Gillespies worked with us until they found more permanent jobs, and it was always enjoyable.

CHAPTER 26

●

The Swimming Hole

Just off the lower corner of the ranch, on the border of two neighboring properties, lies one of the premier play places of the South Fork, where the river drops over a bed of solid granite worn smooth by eons of grinding water and sediment. Judy remembered spending much time here as a child, sliding in the current through drop-offs into pool after pool then over the final waterfall into the whirlpool, or floating in a calm, deep hole with a smooth sandy bottom, or just baking on the rocks in the hot summer sun, then cooling off in the sparkling clear, green water. Now, she was going to get to share this special place with her girls, and look forward to them doing the same with their kids—and the most fun of all was watching the Shatners get to know the swimming hole.

Bill approached this experience as he did all the other things we introduced him to, that is, full speed ahead. Within minutes he was sliding down over the shiny rocks, splashing into the pool at the bottom of the waterfall and emerging laughing and happy. It was good that neither the business office nor his agent was aware of their star trying to mimic the antics of the kids, sliding down the slick bedrock channels standing up, with no protection if he fell. His only disappointment seemed to be that this marvelous play place wasn't located entirely on his property, but had to be shared with the neighbors. He soon got over that, however, when he saw how seldom it was used, and that it was available almost anytime he wanted it, and as he got to know the neighbors he felt better about it.

Summer was a wonderful time, especially for Judy and the girls, as other local family, like Judy's sister Terri and her husband, Leuder, would come and play in the river. One summer Saturday we shared the swimming hole with a group of 12-year olds that were in a Sunday School class I taught in Exeter. After the initial splashing and playing, they gathered on the big rock in the middle of the river for a story. I had arranged with my son, Chris, to go behind them and get in a hole that is covered with water from the current but has a breathing space, like a hidden cavern behind a miniature waterfall. As I told the story of an Indian boy that was lost in the river and never found, I walked around the group and they pivoted to follow me. At a pre-arranged signal Chris stuck his hand up through the falling water, and the kids could see nothing else, just this 12-year-old size hand protruding from the river. For a moment I thought I would have to resuscitate a couple of them, then Chris stood up in view and everyone laughed.

It does get warm, no, hot, in Three Rivers in the summer, and it is the river that saves our minds from being baked. To slip into the cool, green water and feel the oppressive heat drain away is more than just relief, it's therapy. It feels so good to just lay back and let cares be washed away. Conversation smoothes out, muscles relax, minds go blank, and it's time to rest.

Early summer brings an upstream migration of rainbow trout, some years so fat as to resemble panfish and always catchable to those who know where, how, and when to use a fly rod. These trout are a welcome addition to the breakfast menu, and it is so gratifying to land one. The river has virtually no public access, so has not been planted for years. The fish are all native-born and in order to grow up in these cold waters must drift downstream in the winter floods to the lake, then as the water warms in the early summer they swim back upstream to summer haunts. This pattern seems to grow a really lively, healthy, hard-fighting when hooked, good-tasting fish.

One summer I wanted to get Chris to a new area we hadn't fished before because it required crossing a channel of the river that flowed swiftly between two ledges into a deeper hole. In order to get across, I brought a left-over fence board and bridged the gap, hoping we could successfully "walk the plank" to get to the other side. I braced it against the sloping surface of the rock then tried it out. Felt good, solid, and I crossed over and back, then went to get fishing gear and Chris.

We came to the new "bridge" and Chris looked at it dubiously. I was full of confidence, and stepped roughly (should have been gently, dummy) onto the end of the board and it immediately slipped down the sloping rock into the river. I was thrown into the water so quickly I had no chance to do anything but go along, so I held my fly rod high above me as I landed on my back and submerged, then was swept down into the pool below. I surfaced as I drifted across the pool to the shallow water on the far end and climbed out on the rocks.

Chris was laughing so hard he had tears in his eyes. He later delighted in telling how all he could see of Dad was a fly rod and a pair of cowboy boots above the water, being swept merrily downstream. I clamored up the rocky bank, sat down and poured the water out of my boots, climbed up to where he was and we went on fishing down the river, forgetting about fishing the tempting, new area.

Early in the summer, while the water is still cold, is the best fishing, and the only nuisance fish we encountered were an occasional sucker, which didn't ever strike our flies, or the squawfish, or hardhead, which would take a fly once in a great while. It is a real disappointment to hook a heavy fish and get excited about landing it only to realize when it broke the surface that it had bigger scales than trout do and no spots or rainbow stripe on its side.

The girls weren't much into fishing, so I was glad to have the company of Chris and Rufus, my bird dog. Rufus would always want to fetch a fish that was on the line, but seemed to realize it was okay for the fishing net to do that job. He practiced, though, in the swimming hole, trying to catch the minnows that congregated around our legs if we sat on the rock and dangled our feet in the water. We never saw him catch one, but he never did stop trying, always wanting to be ready for an opportunity to help me land a real fish.

CHAPTER 27

●

Trainers

Bill, Christy Wood, ca 1981

There are about as many philosophies about cow horse training methods as there are horse trainers and owners. Everyone seems to have some phase of the method that is different from everyone else. Consequently, when an owner or manager is looking for a trainer for the ranch's horses it is likely that almost everyone will settle for a compromise position in some regard. Our desires were complicated by the involvement of the Shatner name, as every trainer feels there are benefits to bringing along a celebrity name when they show a horse, and some tend to believe that celebrities have endless funds for training, which our budget definitely didn't allow.

We had well-defined desires in looking for someone to be attached to the ranch in the development of our babies. First of all, we were not ready to campaign a horse to a finished cutting or reining prospect, but wanted to put probably 90 days of training on these young horses, just enough to demonstrate a willingness as two-year olds to accept training and to show the beginning of developing athletic ability. We also wanted, if possible, to keep them near the ranch, so we could monitor progress and methods, especially as we were getting acquainted with a trainer.

For the initial handling of our first group of foals we chose a Three Rivers trainer, Christy Wood, of Wood 'n Horse Stables, partly because she was local, but also because we had come to know her as a competent horsewoman. She spent time at the ranch working with the foals to begin handling and ground training, and also worked to teach Bill the finer points of lunging and teaching ground manners. He was a good student, though all trainers think, as said earlier, that their methods excel over all others, and Christy worked to move him to her way of thinking and training, not all of which were familiar to him. He honored her instruction, and did as she taught.

The next year, as our first babies were a year older and ready for some beginning riding, we looked at cutting trainers and located one close by, outside the town of Tulare, by the name of Will Landers. He had trained with Greg Ward, a consistent winner in cutting and reining, and had good references. We outlined to him our desires, and he seemed to fit what we needed, so we took him a couple of horses. He put basic training on these young horses, and as we entered them in chosen sales arenas they handled as well as they should for what training they had. Again, we were not ready to train to show, but just to sell.

By the next year Bill had seen some cuttings, and was enthralled by the skill of these finely trained horses. He decided he would like to try to ride a cutting horse, but wanted a trainer that was closer to Los Angeles, as his time was very limited, and also we both desired to work with one that had demonstrated a higher level of skill by winning at more shows, so we met with Chubby Turner in Santa Ynez. Chubby is one of those cutting horse trainers who has a knack for getting the knowledge inside a horse that it needs to rate a cow properly, to develop its natural athletic ability to roll back and turn quickly, and to refine those cow horse instincts that let the horse do the major decision making on what is needed next to control the cow's movements.

We took Bill and Marcy to Chubby's ranch and they each got to ride a well-trained cutting horse. Both said they loved the experience, but letting the horse do the thinking and much of the decision making seemed foreign to them. They are both well trained equestrians, but their style of riding didn't allow the horse that freedom, since neither had learned that in the cutting arena they can, and must, trust the horse to make the right moves at the right time.

Since the cutting arena activity and the time needed to practice for it didn't seem to suit Bill, the next year we went back to our original plan of just getting the young horses we were raising used to handling and a basic riding experience. It's interesting to see how different the methods are when these young horses are shown at sales. I remember a two-year old cutting/reining prospect from northern Nevada at the Snaffle Bit Futurity Sale in Reno one year that showed as solidly as many mature horses, clear down to a bow to knee level at the end of the exhibition run. Contrasted with this were some prospects trained by Greg Ward and a few others that acted as if they didn't care whether or not the rider even stayed aboard. Greg was well-known for his style of barely breaking, but somehow still really training horses for his style of riding, and had won many shows and competitions, especially in reining. It speaks of the versatility of the cow horse breed, and this became a metaphor for my own development, as I realized that a country boy like me could adapt to conditions and move in circles completely foreign to my upbringing and become comfortable enough to be effective there, even though I was "barely broke" to that environment.

CHAPTER 28

◉

Crystal's Baby

Every horse operation has its triumphs and its failures, and Belle Reve Ranch was no exception to this rule. We had acquired a mare named Crystal Drift Bar, a classic cow-horse built mare, muscular, long hip, nice head, really athletic, and sorrel with a lot of white on legs and face, a beautiful mare. She was well bred, too, being of Doc Bar and Driftwood breeding, both leading cutting horse sires. Crystal's natural athletic abilities promised babies that will perform, and her good looks would put on that extra edge that trainers love. We bred her to a winning cutting stallion of the Freckles line, and eagerly awaited the foal.

When the baby came we were elated—Crystal had produced exactly what we wanted, a sorrel filly with some chrome, muscular from birth, small head, bright eye, and more personality than her mother, if that were possible. She was so cute, and so quick on her feet, and loved running with the other foals in the main pasture between the ranch house and Bill's house where we kept the mares with new babies.

I returned to the ranch one afternoon from a trip to the valley when the filly was probably three months old and, as always, first checked the pasture. All seemed well, everyone was accounted for, and Crystal's baby was lying by the pond, looking at the other foals playing. A short time later I looked again and she was still there, hadn't moved. With a sense of foreboding I walked down near her, and as she struggled to her feet I could see a compound fracture of a front leg. I was devastated.

I called our vet, Dr. Ron Humason of Lone Oak Veterinary Clinic, and told him that we really needed help and described the injury. He sent his main guy, Dr. John Migliore, right up, and his examination simply confirmed what we already knew. While waiting for him to arrive I had called Bill to give him the bad news and get him to concur with any treatment the vet may prescribe, which turned out to be to get the filly to the clinic for reconstructive surgery.

She was still small enough that we were able to get her and her mother in the trailer and transported to the clinic. The prognosis after further examination was quite optimistic, and they put her leg back together. Soon she was recovering, and doing well. We were still cautious, but relieved. It had been quite a few days since the surgery, and she was eating well, getting around, and looking bright-eyed again.

Then came the unexpected but ominous telephone call from the vet—the filly had suddenly died. Talk about an emotional roller coaster ride! I ordered an autopsy, we needed to know why we had lost this battle. The finding was that a blood clot had left the wound/surgery site and traveled to the heart, causing the death. It was nobody's fault, and there was nothing that should have been done differently, it was just the result of one of those risks you live with in the horse business. I still miss that baby.

CHAPTER 29

◉

Wild, Natural Three Rivers

Bear Track in the Road, Lower Grouse Valley

The ranch is on the South Fork of the Kaweah. Just over the hill to the north is the East Fork. It heads in a high elevation valley that had much serious mining activity in the 19th century, and became known as Mineral King. The ore dwindled and now the area has been incorporated into Sequioa National Park, which precludes any more mining activity, but there are still a few privately-owned properties at the edge of the main valley, at about the 7,000 foot level. It is a very popular area for hikers, both day-use and those who park their vehicles and backpack into the really high country to the east, north, or south, including all the way to Mt. Whitney.

There is a real hazard for those who park vehicles at the trailheads, and that is the marmot population. For some reason these critters (call them groundhogs or rockchucks if that is the designation you grew up with) have developed a taste for electrical wiring, radiator hoses, and fan belts on vehicles. Someone told me the insulation on these wires is made with vegetable oil, and apparently they told the rodents too, as they really like to chew on them. A visit to those parking lots shows all kinds of creative use of chicken wire or other deterrents to keep the rodents out of vehicles, some of which work some of the time.

The wonders of Mineral King are worth the risk. In the twenty-five or so mile trip up the hill from Three Rivers to roads' end the environment changes from oak and brush, dry foothills to lush, green meadows with evergreen trees and abundant streams full of trout and lofty, above-timberline crags that majestically pierce the sparkling blue sky. Summer thundershowers keep things green and daytime temperatures are mostly in the 60s and 70s. Winter brings deep snow, with individual storms dumping up to ten feet of snow in a couple of days, laying it in store for the downstream water supply as it slowly melts away late into summer.

One of the last years we were at the ranch my son, Chris, and I went to Mineral King for a couple of days. We camped at a campground for just one night, then made a day trip up the mountain to look for new fishing spots and to see places we hadn't seen before. We hiked light, carrying just a lunch, some water, and our fishing poles, and headed south toward Mineral Lakes, Mosquito Lakes, and Eagle Lake. We caught and released some beautiful brook trout, saw high country that we had previously seen only from a distance, admired the clear, crystalline waters of glacial lakes, and were looked at askance by regulation backpackers because we didn't have the proper gear for an extended stay.

A vivid, Technicolor memory that will stay with me permanently is of a brook trout in the deep, clear waters of the upper Mosquito Lake. I stood on a big rock at the north end of the lake and studied the depths. It was not at all like looking through water, but like the air was just thicker, it was so clear. Suddenly I saw a trout, quietly suspended as if in that thicker air, probably sixty feet out from shore and maybe ten feet deep in the water, several feet above the bottom. I thought, "Wow,

I wonder if I can get him to bite?" I false-casted until there was enough line out, then dropped my fly on the water, some twenty feet short of the trout. It was not a dry fly, so it began to sink slowly, and as it did, the fish spotted it. I saw him start slowly swimming toward the fly, picking up speed as he moved closer. It was a real strain to keep from moving the line, but to let the lure continue to sink slowly toward the level of the fish. He moved deliberately toward my fly, then opened his mouth and bit. Timing my action perfectly, I set the hook, landed the fish, gently removed the barbless hook and turned him loose, thanking him for the wonderful experience. Chris and I continued our hike, newly energized with adrenaline from the success of the whole magical trip.

Our day hike only covered probably seven miles, but took us the full day to travel up 3,000 feet in elevation, from 7,500 to 10,500 and back down to the campground where we started. Needless to say, we were really worn out, but very satisfied with the day.

Directly across the canyon to the north from the ranch, and south of Mineral King, is Case Mountain, the dominant skyline feature in that direction. It has a broad summit with several small peaks at about the 6,800 foot elevation, and has a significant number of sequoia trees. Many of these have been logged in past years, as the area has had, and still does, several privately owned parcels surrounded by BLM land. Road access is from the Mineral King Road, and is also available (to those who have enough keys) from Salt Creek or South Fork Drive. Currently the access is gated and locked off, except to property owners or the CDF fire crews, but when we lived at the ranch it was often open to public access. It is a remarkably short drive to the top of the mountain, and has provided scenic tours for us more than once, as well as one really memorable horseback trip for Judy and some of her friends.

The ladies Judy rides with are often quite adventurous, and spent much of one summer organizing to take a few days' trip to Case

Mountain. Part of the group left from the Salt Creek side, a long, mostly gentle climb on good roads, and others rode in from the South Fork, meeting near the top of the ridge, where they made camp next to a nice pond that furnished water for the horses. The evening was enjoyable, camp was comfortable, especially since a friend had trucked in and stashed at the campsite earlier in the day an ice chest with special refreshments, and the ladies enjoyed a show of lightning and thunder accompanied by a light shower, then chatted quite late into the night before turning in. It seemed they had just got to sleep when they heard a vehicle, and it turned out to be the ice chest owner. He was a firefighter, and told them he had heard on the radio that the lightning had started a fire near them. Pretty soon they heard the sound of fire trucks maneuvering around or over the runoff berms in the road, and soon a fire truck with flashing red lights turned its headlights on the camp and stopped. A voice boomed out, "You'd better head down as soon as it's light, there is a wildfire coming this direction."

Needless to say, there was no more sleep that night, with keeping an eye on the potentially panicking horses and listening to vehicle activity nearby. When daylight arrived, an inspection showed the camp and the horses covered with a fine layer of ash, so there was no question about leaving or staying. They headed for the pond to water the obviously dry horses, and were amazed to see the fire trucks had pumped the water out of the water hole to fight the fire. All that was left was a tiny, wet mudhole right in the middle of the pond. Judy had brought a supply of plastic bags, so she waded through the mud out to where she could scoop the bag full of muddy water, then passed it to one of the others who came part way out, who handed it on to the others like a bucket brigade. They kept this going for what must have been half an hour before the horses had enough of a drink for the trip down the hill, then they exited the area. So much for three days of relaxation on Case Mountain.

We never did see a mountain lion actually on the ranch, or even any definite sign that one had been there, but we knew they were close by. Neighbors had reported seeing lions occasionally, and one year the sightings seemed to be more frequent.

It was that year that we went out to the corrals one morning and found two of our horses bleeding from large scratches on the legs and sides. We never did find definite claw patterns or other identifying characteristics that would define a lion attack, and we do understand it is really rare for a lion to attack a full-grown horse. There was still a barbed-wire fence on one side of the pasture these mares were in, so perhaps they were frightened by a lion or bear walking through and ran into the fence. We'll never know. Both of the horses recovered quickly and nicely, so it was no big deal.

One day I was coming home from work in the Valley quite late, probably nine or ten at night, and as usual, South Fork Drive was deserted. I often would come home without passing anyone on the road after I left the highway, six miles below the ranch. This was a really peaceful drive, and dark with no street lights. I crossed the steel bridge about two miles from home and continued up the hill as usual, enjoying the solitude of the drive, and just as I reached the road that turns off to the houses at 44795 South Fork Drive, there was a mountain lion walking up the road—then, as my headlights moved on, another just ahead of the first one, then, unbelievably, a third lion, all seeming quite nonchalant about my coming up on them.

I put on the brakes to keep from hitting them, and realized that I wouldn't get stopped before passing at least one of the three. The last one in line was the biggest—the others were probably two-thirds grown—and I deduced it was a lioness with her last-year kittens. As I passed the mother, the two young cats trotted off the road and started up the hill. The lioness was behind me now, and turned and walked down the road. I felt quite safe in my car, so on a whim put it in reverse and began backing down the road toward the cat. The combination of brake and back-up lights showed her now trotting down the road, then as I got closer she swerved off the lower side of the road and down over the steep bank out of sight. I coasted to a stop and sat there a few moments, enjoying the wonder of seeing three mountain lions at one time.

I was wondering how much danger there was in lions that were no more afraid of vehicles than these were. Is this a sign that they are also less afraid of humans in general, and therefore more apt to be a problem to livestock, pets, or even to people?

While I sat there pondering these unanswerable thoughts, I was startled to see the lion reappear from the lower side of the road, and with apparently little thought of any danger, walk up the road in the bright headlights toward where the young ones had gone. This was really baffling to me, as my car was parked in the middle of the road, engine running, lights on, window open, my scent not blocked in any way, and she paid no attention to any of this, but continued up the road at a leisurely pace to join the others.

When I arrived home, I told Judy this extraordinary story, and asked her to be careful about security around the ranch, as we had no idea where these lions would roam as mother taught babies how to find things to eat. Over the next few months there were several sightings on the South Fork, all below the bridge where I had seen these. Apparently they didn't travel far enough up the road to be a problem to us.

One of the more interesting scavengers around Three Rivers is the raccoon. These nocturnal animals are seldom seen, but leave their distinctive footprints in dust or mud as they travel through looking for things to eat. Sometimes at night our dog would bark, but we weren't sure why.

One morning as I started toward the barn for early morning rounds, the dog (Rufus) was sitting on the paver bricks in front of the house looking intently up at the gingko tree. About two thirds of the way to the top of the tree was a very worried-looking raccoon. Rufus was proud to have it treed, and thought we should do something with it. I called the family to come admire it, then went on to the barn, taking Rufus with me. By the time I got back an hour or so later, the tree was empty. All the masked marauder needed was a little space to make his escape.

Three Rivers has two kinds of deer, the Whitetail and the California Blacktail, the latter being the most common. These are smaller than the mule deer I was used to seeing in Idaho, and had smaller ears, but otherwise were very similar, especially in habits.

One day as Judy and I drove down the South Fork, we saw a deer, a doe, on the road and slowed to pass it safely. As we approached it the deer didn't run, but turned to face us, and as I stopped, it came over and sniffed at the open window as if expecting a treat. Judy suggested it must be the one that belonged to Jill and Cal Johnson, or at least it had adopted them when its mother had been killed on the road and they had kept it from starving to death. Jill named it Robin. She lived at their ranch for her entire life, and was the topic of many conversations, especially among the tourists that happened on her, who were invariably enthralled by being able to spend time close to a live deer.

At the ranch, the deer were a pest in the garden. It was really difficult to keep them from eating those tender plants that humans like also, and they always seemed to feed on the ones we were expecting to eat next. I had been raised on a ranch in Idaho where deer were a staple in our diet, and one year I decided that it would be a good idea to harvest one of those nicely fattened animals—after all, it spent enough time there to be considered garden produce. I was in the habit of keeping a current hunting license, so I crept out of the house with my gun in the early morning light, found a deer in the garden, and bagged it. Like I had been used to doing in Idaho I turned it over to field dress it and get it ready for butchering, and was astonished to see the belly of that pretty animal just covered with ticks and lice. That was nothing like I knew in Idaho, where there is enough winter to control those pests. It sure wasn't very appetizing, but I finished the butchering process and got the deer safely into the freezer. It never did taste right to me, and I haven't had a desire to hunt a California deer since that experience.

Bears occasionally came to the ranch, but caused no more problems than some barking by the dog and a few broken branches on fruit trees as they loved to eat the fruit. We never did see one inside the fence.

CHAPTER 30

●

Wedding Reenactment

As the tenth anniversary of Bill and Marcy's wedding neared, they informed us that they were holding a reenactment of that day, were going to recite vows again, and invited us to their home in Studio City for the party. It was to be a formal event, and we started preparing for a celebrity-studded affair.

Judy shopped for two days to find the proper western-styled dress to represent us as horse people, and I found a tuxedo rental place (no, I didn't, and still don't, own one) that had a western-styled tux, and I had recently purchased a pair of chocolate brown colored alligator classic western boots. The look was perfect. I remember a couple of compliments I received at that party about how perfect the outfit was. I was flattered to think that I had impressed Hollywood folk.

Bill's house was a perfect party place, with a nice, private back yard that included a hardwood cover for the pool that made it a great dance floor. The affair was catered by the best, and I was introduced for the first time to coconut shrimp (remember I grew up on a small farm in Idaho, a long ways from shrimp country) and other things I still can't name, but really enjoyed. I wasn't a bit bashful about getting my share of all of them.

We met a bunch of celebrities, including Leonard Nimoy and most of the original Star Trek crew, Heather Locklear and others of T. J. Hooker, and a smattering of others that I didn't recognize, as I never have been much of a follower of the movie crowd.

Bill and Marcy were the perfect host and hostess, making sure we were introduced to anyone that mattered, and not neglected. We came away feeling that not only were they good people, but they cared about us.

CHAPTER 31

◉

Saddlebreds

G riffith Park Equestrian Center in Los Angeles is near the studio where Bill did a lot of filming, and he would go there to ride occasionally when he didn't have time to come to Three Rivers. While there he became acquainted with an old horseman, Royce Cates, who was deeply involved in the training and showing of American Saddlebred horses. Marcy loved to go to those stables, too, and was drawn to the showy way the gaited horses traveled and to Royce's old west manner. It wasn't long before Marcy was asking Bill to invest in some Saddlebreds, since they already had a ranch where the horses could be kept.

Apparently the size of the Saddlebred business as compared to the quarter horse world had an effect on Bill's thinking, as he found that with a relatively minimal investment he could become an influential part of that world. We had been in the quarter horse business a few years and were still quite anonymous except for a growing circle of friends and acquaintances, since that business is so big. Also, Bill was working regularly now, and was in a better position financially to invest, so invest they did, buying a stable full of mares and then a stallion. Soon they added more (we never did know exactly how many) and before long Bill explained that they had purchased a ranch in Kentucky (and named it Belle Reve Farm) to keep those horses on and use as a base for showing those they trained, but would also bring some to pasture on the ranch in Three Rivers at times. I think Judy and I were a little unsettled about this from the beginning—not so much that we were not consulted about Bill branching out into that business, but that it would interfere with the quarter horse operation since pasture space was limited and we were counting on some profits sometime. It was with a sense of uncertainty that we watched for the first Saddlebreds to arrive.

Bill and Marcy brought Royce to the ranch to get acquainted. While there Royce informed us that in the spring he would be bringing some Saddlebred mares and their foals to graze here, and gave us his philosophy of raising the babies. Contrary to what we did with the quarter horse foals, he didn't want the babies to have any human contact while young. When they were yearlings, he said, they could be touched, but only for doctoring and hoof trimming. Strange, we thought, but they were his project, and we would go along with whatever he wished. It was somewhat of an adjustment in our thinking to see those funny looking (to us) long-legged mares alongside our stocky quarter horses. We never did confess to Bill that Judy's descriptions included slab-sided, cow-hocked, beady little eyed, pigeon-mouthed, and brainless, among other derogatory terms. Probably most of that stemmed from the mare that deliberately walked up behind Judy and bit her on the shoulder. Besides, we quarter horse people really are narrow-minded about the muscular physiques and super-intelligent eyes of the quarter horses we have grown to love.

Because of the extra acreage we had acquired, there was room in good, irrigated pastures for these extra horses. We kept them separated from the quarter horse mares, and things went pretty well, but I never could get my mind around the mentality of those mares. For instance, one day I was watching from outside the main pasture that held probably six or eight mares and foals when they suddenly started running across the pasture. They headed for the closed gate at the other side of the pasture, then circled uphill when nearing the gate and the fence. Except for one young mare, that is.

We had built these fences with heavy, treated posts and a single rough-cut 2x6 along the top of five-foot no-climb horse wire. I was about to see a demonstration of the strength of this construction, as this mare just kept cantering toward the gate, then at the last minute, too late to make the corner, turned the way the other mares had gone and seeing there was no way to make the corner, jumped into the air in a twisting maneuver, and hit the fence with her shoulder. The heavy board flexed, the post held, the horse bounced off and went on after her friends with no apparent ill effects to the horse or the fence. Why? I have no idea what motivates an animal to deliberately vault into a fence like that. I am just very grateful it was not regular wire, or light boards, or so many other materials that could have caused injury.

In summary, our Saddlebred experiences were not pleasant enough to convince us that they were more likeable than our beloved quarter horses, even if Bill and Marcy did think so. Perhaps there was a clue there to the future of our association with the ranch, but apparently we missed it at the time.

CHAPTER 32

A Missing Baby

It was spring again, and all the mares were foaling, including the Saddlebreds. We brought one Saddlebred mare in to the foaling corral between the house and the barn where we could watch her more closely. I would check on her all through the night, and a couple of days later when I got up in the morning she seemed agitated, striding around the pen. As I watched her, it occurred to me that she didn't look pregnant anymore, she was suddenly thin again. There was no baby in the pen, no other signs of a birth, yet the mare had definitely foaled. I recalled some whinnying in the night, but when I got up then and checked, all seemed normal. One of the quarter horse mares in the pasture across a lane was showing undue interest in all of this, trotting up and down the fence, but that in itself wasn't unusual at foaling time, so I had gone back to bed.

A quick look in the pen, and then a trip around the ranch showed no signs of a baby. All the obvious conclusions were brought up and discounted (mountain lions, etc.) and there was still no reason for a baby horse to just disappear. I looked for tracks in the dusty road. I checked the fence again. I reexamined the mare. Nothing made any sense. I leaned on the fence and just stood there, trying to think of something. Nothing came to mind except how were we going to explain to Bill and Royce that this mare wasn't really pregnant and didn't foal at all? In disgust I just left the corral and walked around the house to get away from the thought of these problems for a while.

Behind the house grows a large pine tree and assorted shrubbery. One of the large, thick shrubs, taller than I am, grows right next to the board fence of the main pasture. For some reason I walked over to the fence by that shrub and as I reached out to lean on the fence, saw movement by the shrub. What?—there, lodged in between the bushy shrub and the board fence was a skinny little hind end of a horse. Moving the brush aside, I pushed through to the front of the little backside, put my arm around its neck, and backed out a newborn foal. It had traveled along the fence until the branches of the shrub stopped it and it just didn't know how to back out of where it was.

Apparently the mare had foaled next to the fence on the downhill side of the pen, and the baby had rolled underneath. From there it had followed along the fence next to the mare in the pasture across the lane until it got stuck in the "no reverse gear" mode behind the bush. It took a while to get the mother to accept it back, but after some work she did, and all was well. Yes, I did block off the space under the bottom fence board so that it could not happen again.

CHAPTER 33

●

Real Horses Think

Bill on Dandy, leading Wicked Witch Fea

Quarter horse people get fanatic about the horses we love, and Bill never did move his thinking to that allegiance like Judy and I had. It seems his personality (and especially that of Marcy) was most suited to the way the Saddlebreds show. Although he did some years later do some riding in reining shows, he didn't spend any time at it while we were at the ranch. We think this was mostly because his riding style never did fit the cow horse mentality, as I had earlier stated.

In order for a rider to win consistently in the cow horse events, especially cutting, he has to accept that the horse is going to do much, if not most, of the decision making as to what needs to be done next to control the cow. For those who ride gaited horses it is a real leap to get to this mindset, as the gaited horse needs constant direction, like an actor. In a cutting contest, or for the cow work in a reining show, the rider must put his hand that holds the reins down on the cutting horse's neck and leave the reins slack while the horse controls the movements of the cow for long enough to show the judges that it is the horse that is doing the thinking. The successful cutting horse rider is the one that has enough trust in the training that the horse has been given, and in the horse itself, to let it do its job. From this unique concept of riding comes the quarter horse lover's saying, "Real horses think."

Judy and I were long spoiled by the mentality and entertaining antics of our horses, including the ranch horses. The horse that William Shatner bought by mistake turned out to be a wonderful horse for the ranch. He was not "finished" in his training, speaking as a true horseman or bridle person would, but was trained well enough to be really fun to ride, responsive to the bit and full of life. When Judy and I rode around the ranch or up the canyon, I usually chose to ride Dandy. If the hill was steep I could feel his powerful hind quarters push us surely up the slope.

One day we had ridden up Grouse Creek in the bottom of the canyon instead of up the road, which gave us an opportunity to explore. We crossed over the creek and rode through the scattered blue oaks up the gentle slopes along the side of the canyon, until the hills got too steep to comfortably pick our way through the rocks. I had ridden off the trail we were following and up the hill slightly to go around some big rocks, and Judy turned to look at where I was just as I unknowingly rode over a yellow jacket nest, and they began streaming out of the ground and stinging Dandy on his tender underside. He pushed hard with those big back legs and the sudden move made me lose my balance. I clung to the saddle horn and struggled in vain to get upright as he took us around the steep hillside, bucking higher each time he was stung. We traveled precipitously close to trees and rocks, and as the side hill became even steeper, I feared that we were going to hit a tree or Dandy would slip on a big, hidden rock and fall with us, as he was not yet really experienced in mountain riding.

I still had not found my balance. I'm not a bronc rider, and decided that instead of trying to cling to the saddle I would feel much safer on the ground, so I took my boots out of the stirrups and let the next lunge push me off the upper side. The fall was minor, we were out of the territory of the bees, and the landing was easy. Dandy went a couple more jumps then stopped and looked back as if to wonder why I had got off. I remounted and we turned and rode back down the canyon side, giving a wide berth to the nest of bees.

The mare Judy most enjoyed riding was Cookie. She had been given to Judy by her sister Terri because she was scared of Cookie's lively ways. Judy grew to really enjoy riding her, as she had plenty of life and personality. Cookie was the source of much entertainment, one example being that she loved to eat apricots. We discovered this when we went out to pick the ripening fruit and there were none on the lower branches. Under the tree near the fence was a pile of apricot pits, neatly stripped of fruit, and we had no idea who had put them there. We kept watch, and it wasn't long before Cookie was standing in the shade of the tree, lazily switching her tail to keep the flies off, and seemed to be eating. Then we saw her reach up, pick a ripe apricot, chew off the fruit, and casually drop the pit onto the growing pile on the ground. We laughed at the sight of that tiny pit coming out of those big lips and Cookie reaching for another fruit.

We think Cookie was half Arabian, and probably the other half was Quarter Horse, though nobody knew for sure. We do know she had the Arabian characteristic of her brain disconnecting now and then, the most memorable example being when she ran away not long after we brought her to the ranch.

Judy would let her loose in the yard to eat sometimes, and one day she just suddenly took off at a gallop down the driveway. We still have no idea what started this mad dash to freedom. I listened to her hoofbeats all the way to the paved county road, then heard a gap in the rhythm as she jumped the cattle guard, heard the clatter of horse shoes on the bridge, and then they faded into the distance, still on the run. We just stood there in unbelief that she would run away.

Judy got a halter and said, "We better go find her," and I said, "Let's take a saddle, I'll ride her back." We loaded tack into the truck and headed down the road. About a mile away from home, there stood Cookie, casually eating grass in a neighbor's pasture that had an open gate. We stopped, Judy walked right up to her, and she was calm and cool about being caught. We put my saddle on her, I mounted up, and we galloped almost all the way back to the ranch. She seemed happy and content to be home, and never ran away again.

CHAPTER 34

Revising a TJ Hooker Script

While Bill was filming for the "TJ Hooker" series, his time was limited, but he still managed to occasionally visit the ranch. One weekend visit included his two Doberman dogs, two that had little exposure to country living and had spent very little time outside a kennel, and probably none off a leash. He took them for a tour of the ranch, introduced them to our dog, Rufus, and they got along okay.

That afternoon Bill spent some time in his house and left the dogs free to run outside, since Rufus lived outside and was fine. When he came out he called the dogs, but nobody came. We heard him calling, and asked where the dogs were. He had no idea, so we began scouring all the pastures, looking and calling. We looked in literally every possible location, knowing they were not country dogs, but not imagining they would leave with Bill there. We crossed the south fence and went up the hill above Grouse Creek, but still no sign of his Dobermans. When it came time for evening chores, I took care of the horses and then we looked some more.

Bill was getting really distraught. He had heard stories of pets traveling cross country for amazing distances to get home, and didn't want to think he would have to wait days or weeks for his dogs to return. We went to the east pasture, then to the house next door, where no one was home. Still he called; still no answering bark or happy dog. Then, on a whim, we looked in a wood shed beside the house on the neighboring ranch, and there, cowering in apparent fear of the wide open spaces of the out-of-doors, were the city-bred dogs. They seemed as glad to see Bill as he was to find them, and they happily went home. All was well again, we thought.

Next time Bill came to the ranch, he asked if we had watched the episode of "Hooker" that was filmed the week after the dog incident. It seems that somewhere in our scouring the hillsides looking for the missing Dobermans Bill had gotten in some poison oak, and his arm broke out in a big rash. Delaying filming of "Hooker" was not an option, so the screen writers made up a story of how Bill had injured his arm (sorry, I don't remember the details of that story) and he appeared with the arm covered in a bandage. Hollywood can adjust, if necessary.

CHAPTER 35

●

Full-time Work & Part-time Work

Now that we had been at the ranch a few years, it was evident that the Idaho business was not going to bring us what we had hoped to relieve the debt burden we were still carrying and give some stepping stones to a future. Randy had determined he was moving to another city and would not be buying the office, but began to prepare to close it and move away. Besides this setback, the buyer of our house had come on hard times and walked away, just like the earlier one had, so we took it back again. Once more we cleaned it up and put it on the market. My California real estate license wasn't producing what I needed, there just wasn't time in my life to put enough effort into that business to build it.

One day I saw an ad in the newspaper for a Realty Officer for the City of Tulare Redevelopment Agency. It was only a 40-mile commute, so I applied, and was offered the job. I went to work full-time to see if that would keep us going. By now the ranch was through the main building stage, and maintenance was becoming more routine, so Judy and the girls, with a little help, were keeping up. I went to Tulare five days a week and was grateful for a steady, reliable paycheck. The working conditions were okay, the associates in the small office were personable and capable, and things moved smoothly, even though I was stretched a little thin by doing ranch chores early mornings and after work as well.

We had been haunted from time-to-time by the prospect of an occupation that I could work at from the ranch, but everything we looked at was either not real or was of a nature that we just didn't feel we could fit in. A friend introduced us to an organization called after the founder, A. L. Williams. The company sold life insurance and investments under some pretty unique ideas, including a networking concept for building individual businesses, and we decided to give it a try. The licensing was easy, and meetings to organize marketing groups were held weekly, with "upline" helpers available as needed to build a business. We made some early progress, some money, some promotions, and were encouraged. Maybe this was it. Now I was devoting some evenings each week to this, and I stretched even thinner. Oh, well, we decided, we can do anything needed for 90 days, then we'll look at our progress. It gave us greater rewards more quickly than the real estate business had, so that cheered us.

The time spent at the ranch, even though the chores were really work, became even more valuable and desirable to me as "retreat" time to rejuvenate my soul. I realized my spiritual progress, including time with Judy, was still the most important part of my life, and we worked hard when it was time to work, then played hard together, our love building and sustaining us in this fast-paced life. Summer became extra special, as my kids came from their home in Nevada to play in the river and let me spend time with them. The ranch became for us the kind of place we visualized building for Bill, one that gave needed breaks from the stresses of that outside life, and healing souls neglected almost daily in the grind of providing temporal things. We were encouraged again.

CHAPTER 36

●

A Few Particular Memories

Crooked Streak (DocOTheBay) in the pasture

We had a few favorites among the babies we raised. One of the early foals of Miss Sheila Bay, a granddaughter of Old Granddad, was sired by Montana Doc. This filly had a name chosen by Judy early on, "Doc O' the Bay," but we called her Crooked Streak, because the strip in her face kind of wandered from side to side on the way down to her nose. Crooked Streak was one of those horses that have no enemies, just friends, and had no fear of anyone. When we went into the pasture she was the first to greet us and get rubbed, or have fly repellant wiped on, or just talked to. Any attention was meaningful and well received. We didn't carry a pocket full of treats, as some owners do, because we wanted the babies to come to us because they liked us, not because we gave them goodies. It worked well, but especially well with Crooked Streak. When it came time to take her to a sale, it was like selling one of our kids (except that she brought more cash than a kid would) and we really hated to see her go.

One of the contemporaries of Crooked Streak was one we called "The Fence Sitter," because of a peculiar habit she had of stepping up on the lower rail of our wooden fences to get a better look across the fence, or at anything. I don't remember her parentage for sure, but I think she was by Broadway Doc. It was strange to look out on the pasture and see the mares and foals gathered by the fence, with one head sticking far above the others, getting a good look over the fence.

One stud colt by Broadway Doc out of a Rocky Knox mare we named Rocky Doc Knox, as I remember. He was built really well, so we delayed gelding him until later than most, in hopes that someone would want a stud prospect. We wanted to put some training on him as a two-year old, so I loaded him into the horse trailer and headed for Will Landers' place. As we rounded the bend over the Horse Creek bridge, I felt the truck sway, then bounce up and down, and couldn't decide what was going on in the trailer. I looked in the rear view mirror and saw, to my horror, a hoof and lower leg sticking out the newly broken window above the feed manger of the trailer. Frantically I pulled over and opened the escape door beside Rocky. He had both front feet in the manger, with the one protruding out the front window—I have no idea to this day how he ducked his head and neck low enough to accomplish that while rearing the front of his body high enough to get both legs in the manger.

I was alone, and knew it was up to me to get Rocky in a position to ride the rest of the way to Tulare. Talking to Rocky to get his legs down as if he could understand me, I lifted on his legs and all at once he reared again, again with his head down, and both front hooves plopped down on the floor in their proper places. A quick examination showed a couple of scratches, but no visible bruising or other problems. He rode quietly the rest of the way, and subsequent training showed he had no ill effects from his acrobatics.

To prove that Rocky could sire a foal, we bred him to a ranch mare when he was still only a two year old. The chance to experience a stud colt growing into early maturity was interesting, as Rocky got a whole different mindset about life, learning to listen to training even though his hormones were asking him to go a different direction. The breeding experiment worked, but he didn't show as much promise in training as we hoped, so we gelded him. Some cowboys reading this may take note, as there are things to be learned from all those around us, human or not.

There was an informal contest for the most beautiful baby each year, and we were not bashful at looking at the other end of the spectrum, either. Honors for the most homely of the babies we raised would be tied between "Benito Burrito" and "Baby Blue Eyes". We bought at a sale one year a mare that was in foal to a stud named Benito San. He had sired some good, performing horses and we felt confident it would be a nice baby. When foaling time came, we saw a little, brown animal with ears like a jack rabbit. We couldn't help but name it "Benito Burrito" in honor of those ears. He did grow into them somewhat, but that first image remained with us.

We had a big, long-legged mare named King's Waspy Gal, a granddaughter of the great quarter horse sire, King. We bred her to Mr Gunsmoke, expecting a wonderful baby. Again, we were surprised. The baby had her mother's long legs, but the nose was matching, probably the longest I've ever seen in a quarter horse. To add to the caricature-like appearance, this filly had one white eye. We sold her as a yearling at the Wexler sale, not willing to keep her any longer.

Judy seemed to have a special attraction for the ranch animals. I remember one visit of Bill's when he was walking up the road to the barn just at feeding time, and saw Judy on her way down the lane to the barn. She was walking nonchalantly along with the dog just behind her, several cats following the dog, and across the pasture fence a line of horses, young and old, all following Judy. Bill began to laugh and called out, "You look just like 'Mother Earth' with her animal friends!" From that time on he often referred to her as 'Mother Earth'.

The ranch dog, Rufus, had some special talents that we enjoyed showing off. He was a retriever, and lived up to that. He seemed to understand more English than many humans do. Judy discovered his talent by accident one afternoon. She had crossed the upper pool at the swimming hole and was sitting on the rock in between the two main slide currents. This was before she had stopped smoking, and she realized she had left her cigarettes on the bank. Nonchalantly she said, "Rufus, get my cigarettes."

As if he understood perfectly what she had said, Rufus got up and started toward her towel and other things she had left behind. I laughed at this, because when Rufus crossed the river it was with a great leap that brought complete immersion, then he swam vigorously to the other bank. I could visualize Judy's cigarettes falling apart in the water-filled package. But I was astonished as he gently picked up her cigarette package, walked to the edge of the river, stepped carefully off the rock into the pool and swam to Judy, the parcel held proudly above the water. As we watched in astonishment, he delivered it to her without any problem. Then, as if it was the ordinary thing to do, she said, "Get my lighter, you forgot it." And he did, the routine being the same. I just stared and laughed. It's scary when your kids learn to understand English, but when your pets do, it's downright frightening.

Rufus loved living at the ranch, and especially liked the trips up the canyon where he could run alongside the horses and explore and sniff as we rode.

I was often busy with ranch work, and Judy rode without me sometimes. One day she had gone riding alone and a couple of hours later came galloping down the Grouse Valley road yelling for help. "Rufus is caught in a coyote trap," she shouted as she rode up. I asked where, jumped on the ATV, and headed up the hill. As I neared the area where I expected to find Rufus I saw him coming down the side of the road, dragging a trap that had him by the toe. It had to be really painful to wrestle it loose from its anchors and head for home.

Having been around and/or using traps all my life, I thought it was no big deal to take it off. I stopped, petted and sympathized with Rufus, then bent down to open the trap. As I put enough pressure on the springs to release the jaws, the trap twisted slightly, and it must have hurt, for Rufus, with a nasty snarl, snapped and bit at my arm. The trap did release, Rufus was free, but I was dumbfounded that he would turn on me, his best friend and obvious benefactor, and try to hurt me. Hadn't I just saved him from further pain and taken away the cause of his hurt? Rufus was immediately grateful to be out of the trap and was obviously sorry that he snapped at me, so I forgave him, of course.

Since that incident, I have tried to keep in mind that I can't always measure the degree of distress that may be in another's system, whether physical or otherwise, and when they turn on me viciously it may be that the problem isn't with me at all, but is because of things going on inside them, sometimes unseen to those around them. This thought makes it easier, even almost automatic, to forgive and overlook entirely any seemingly offensive words or actions.

Bird dogs get old, just like all of us do, and after a few years at the ranch we began to realize how old Rufus was. He had come with us from Idaho, and had enjoyed a wonderful, full life. I still tell Judy occasionally that in the next life I want to be her bird dog, to be loved like Rufus was loved, and treated like he was. When his life was over, we wanted him to be part of the ranch, so I picked a special place on the Grouse Creek side of the pasture, and buried him there. I used the tractor to move a big, granite rock over the top of his grave and then chiseled an "R" into the face of it.

Many years later, Sal Natoli, the current caretaker of the ranch, asked me about a big rock that he had discovered in the lower pasture that had an "R" on its side. He was pleased to know the story of Rufus.

CHAPTER 37

Bill's Embarrassing Moments

B ill was pretty familiar with horses, including experience with horses on the sets of some movies, and one of the things he really looked forward to was "humanizing" a foal, that is, getting a new baby to accept a human presence and submit to training, even right after its birth. When a mare foaled, he wanted to be called right away, so if his schedule permitted, he could come to the ranch and spend time with the baby. He did get to come up and welcome some babies, surrounding them with loving arms and cooing soft words, and it probably was good for them, but we couldn't always tell. Foals of the cow horse breeding we liked were naturally of a gentle disposition anyway.

One especially perky filly seemed to be a favorite of Bill's, even though she was out of an Appaloosa ranch mare, not a quarter horse. On one of his ranch visits he climbed over the wooden fence into the pasture, wanting to get her to eat out of his hand. We had a "creep feeder" for the foals, one that was built so the babies could get in but the mares couldn't, and we kept it filled with tasty and nutritious growth feeds the foals really liked. Bill thought that if he got some of that feed the foal would eat out of his hand, figuratively and literally. He got some feed, then stood between the feeder and the baby, thinking she would get the idea. Apparently she didn't want to cooperate, and kept trying to get around him. He would move to stay in front of her, outstretched hands full of feed, squatting down to be on her level. She put up with his attentions for some time, but as Judy and I watched we could see her getting more restless, and Bill had to be more agile to stay between the filly and the feeder where she wanted to be. We warned him that the baby had had enough, but he wanted to keep trying. He didn't have a rope or halter on her, but kept moving around to block her path, wanting her to eat from his hands. He can be really persistent—doing retakes until it is done right seems to be second nature to him. It seemed to us that the filly was getting really tired of all this attention, but he kept on.

As the filly dodged to try to get around him, Bill shuffled over to block her path, when suddenly the filly whirled and kicked out, rear hooves catching Bill right in the crotch, then she trotted off happily into the pasture. Bill dropped the feed, scrambled over the pasture fence, collapsed on the ground, and just sat there for a few minutes with a really distressed look on his face, which turned to a wry smile as he started to chuckle, realizing the filly had educated him instead of the other way around.

One beautiful spring day Bill came to visit the ranch, followed by a reporter and a photographer from People Magazine. Bill announced that they wanted to do an article that included some photos of him riding, and he wanted to ride Dandy, the really good looking ranch gelding. We thought that was a fine idea, but cautioned Bill that Dandy hadn't been ridden very much recently and he may be feeling a little frisky.

We caught Dandy and brought him to be saddled, when Bill said, "Why can't I ride bareback?" Nobody had any knowledge of whether Dandy had been ridden bareback before, but he insisted, so we said, "Let's try it," and gave him a leg up. Bill rode down the road past the barn, then turned around and trotted up for the photographer. The photographer asked that this be repeated, then again. This was fine for Bill, he was used to retakes, and was really enjoying the rides, but Dandy didn't understand the why of these energetic trips to nowhere.

It seemed to him that they should be going farther, or at the least going somewhere. Judy and I could see Dandy getting quite agitated, but Bill didn't seem to mind. He was apparently keyed in to the camera, not to the horse. We warned him that this was probably enough, that Dandy was too fresh and edgy to continue, but he wanted to do one more trip.

As they approached the barn on a brisk trot, Dandy apparently thought it would be better if they could cover more ground and get this nonsense over with, so he broke into a canter. That felt so good to him that he let his powerful hind quarters give an enthusiastic thrust or two and Bill, with no saddle on, came unattached. He landed not at all gracefully on his back on the road right in front of the photographer, and the reporter and the photographer loved it.

When the next issue of People came out, it had the promised article, including a photo of Bill landing on his back in the road. The truth was ignored in the photo caption that told how much Bill enjoyed doing his own stunt work. Such is Hollywood.

CHAPTER 38

●

Watching a TJ Hooker Filming

During a visit to the business office, Victor suggested I may want to watch a scene in the filming of TJ Hooker, one in which a car crashes into a stack of glass five-gallon water bottles. He made arrangements for some of us to be there, and on the way would have lunch at one of the "in" hamburger places near the office.

The pre-lunch conversation turned out to be a real eye-opener for this country boy. I have not always led a totally sheltered life, but will admit to my worldly experience being quite limited. Here I was, sitting with a group of the upper echelon of Hollywood and Los Angeles people, and suddenly vulgar words and phrases were being used in conversation as if this were the normal way to converse. I was shocked to find that those who could be looked up to as leaders of society were lacking in common decency, it seemed to me. Since that day I have pondered on this, and find that life is sweeter and more pleasant, and it is easier to keep a positive, less-antagonistic outlook on life if we eliminate those words and phrases from our conversations. It is to me a sign of mental immaturity to need to rely on the "shock factor" to make a point. I still look on the conversations of that day with sorrow for the growth of those generations who follow.

After lunch we went to the filming location and found a spot out of camera view, but near enough to get a good look at what was going on. Suddenly, around the corner came a speeding automobile, and it crashed into the stack of bottles, with glass and water flying. As it came to a stop, the stunt man driver sprang out of the car, vaulted the block wall the bottles were stacked against, and disappeared across the adjoining yard.

The magic of film making was never demonstrated so clearly to me as at this time, for what we had seen happen in an instant was over so quickly that it was no big thing, yet when I watched the slow-motion shots on the actual broadcast, it was emphasized to become a real crash and a major scene. Hollywood has learned how to make little things look really big, and vice-versa, as I thought about the language at lunch.

CHAPTER 39

———————— • ————————

Handgun Practice

Bill didn't visit the ranch often, especially as his career took off again and he was busy filming the TJ Hooker series, then the Star Trek movies. When he did visit, it was often a spur-of-the-moment thing, sometimes without any notice he was coming, or maybe a request like "Can you get the house dusted, I'll be there tomorrow?" Also, since we hardly ever visited, and didn't read the Hollywood news or scandal sheets, we were usually the last to know any news of him, whether regarding career or personal life, so we had no way of guessing if his life was going well or was in a turmoil.

On one of these impromptu visits, he hardly said hello, then went to the house and we didn't see him for some time. We began to wonder if all was okay, but recognized that he is a grownup, has a life to live, and definitely should be allowed his own space to do whatever he feels like. After all, it is his property.

In the afternoon, we heard gunfire, close by, and went to the edge of the pasture to see what was going on. There was Bill, automatic pistol in hand (nice one, too) practicing his marksmanship. To this day, we have no knowledge if he likes guns or was practicing for some role he was playing. We watched briefly from a distance, just enough to see that he was careful about the safety of the horses and anyone else, and he was, so we went on with what we were doing. Soon he disappeared into the house again, and all was quiet. That was a day trip; he was just there for a few hours then back to LA.

CHAPTER 40

———————— • ————————

Baby in the Rain

One of the mares that seemed really well suited to having babies was a Buddy Leo mare, leggy, smooth moving, one of those easy-striding, ground-covering horses. We didn't use her for riding, even though it was tempting, but bred her and watched for the baby to see which of her desirable characteristics were passed on to the foal.

Because of the AQHA ruling that all foals born in a calendar year were considered the same age, with an assigned birth date of January 1, we bred to get foaling as early in the year as possible. January through March is generally the wettest time of the year in Three Rivers, so we arranged a larger stall in the barn for those mares closest to foaling. The problem is, you can't always tell exactly when a foal is coming, so it is a guess which mare needs to be in the stall first. To watch them closely, we put smaller corrals near the house, from which we would move the mares to the barn when indications were that it was time.

Buddy was in one of these corrals waiting for time to be moved in the barn. We checked on the mares as evening came on, then decided to go to town for a movie. While we were gone it rained vigorously, and on our return, as the headlights shined into the small corrals all seemed well except I had a feeling that Buddy needed a visit. I put on raingear, got a flashlight and went out for a closer look. Buddy came to the fence to greet me as usual, and as I shined the light across the corral I could see a lump in the middle of a large pool of rainwater. My heart dropped; I vaulted the fence, and sure enough, it was a new baby, shaped like a horse but in the habitat of a frog. As I approached it lifted its head and I breathed a sigh of relief as I gathered it up and carried it into the warm, dry stall, with Buddy following anxiously behind me. After it had been toweled off it happily attached to Buddy for a snack, and all was well.

Is there a scientific explanation why many mares seem stimulated to foal in a storm? I've asked many horsemen this question, and nobody seems to have a credible answer. One said it had to do with atmospheric pressure. Another thought that it was a defense mechanism left over from when horses ran wild, that if the foal dropped during a storm the scent of foaling was washed away to keep predators from finding it. Some just shake their heads and say something about human females and unpredictability. I'd still like to know.

CHAPTER 41

———— • ————

Enticed Away

The ALW business provided a fast track to some growth for us, and we were very encouraged by the progress made. I quit the City of Tulare (prematurely, it proved) to devote more time to keeping my real estate office working and still building the insurance/investment business. Soon I was a local leader in ALW and doing well some months, then our team would disappear, or change, or just quit, and we would be back to starting over. It was in that period of time that I should have realized my lack of social skills, my shortage of local connections, and the remoteness of living at the ranch could be fatal to this type of business, but since optimism is such an integral part of networking, I kept convincing myself it would work. We attended conventions, and again I should have been able to see how ill-fitting my personality and circumstances were to what we were trying to do, but apparently I refused to look at what was really happening. There were clues I should have picked up on, such as groups of people gathered around certain leaders at conventions or meetings, animated conversations going on that generated high enthusiasm, and other sociality that I was able to observe because I spent time alone, watching. The obvious went right over my head, that I didn't enjoy the "groupie" mentality that made for a successful team. It wasn't until much later that I faced up to this reality and got out of that business.

We would not allow the ranch to suffer, and we didn't, but we suffered. It was too demanding a schedule, the real estate business still had huge demands and Idaho reared its head again to demand some attention. Randy had completed his move to Idaho Falls, and that finished the closing of the real estate office. For the third time we sold the Idaho house, and this time it was to a qualified buyer who obtained financing, and it was finally out of our life. The great relief that sale provided was somewhat overshadowed by the stresses of California, but it was our last Idaho burden. Now we could concentrate all our energies here, and our focus became: family and relationship first, ranch next, then real estate and ALW. It was at least some progress.

While we were at the ranch life had gone on. Our girls were both married, and had moved away to start their own lives. Our first grandson, Garrett Good, had come and showed promise of being a baseball star, based on how early and how well he learned to throw the ball. Both the girls and their growing families lived quite close by, so we were able to spend time together. Family is great.

CHAPTER 42

◉

Sex & Violence

As if prostituting our mares out to the top stallions were not enough, it seems to be a Hollywood legacy that every script must have some sex, violence, and a love triangle, and this one is no exception. First, the sex.

Dandy, the ranch gelding, had been kept a stallion until after breeding some mares, and then was gelded. The act of being gelded later in life not only contributed much to his masculine good looks, but also apparently left some vivid and fond memories of past actions. We didn't realize this until the spring after he came to the ranch and some mares began coming into heat. It wasn't a problem, he was completely controllable, but it was also extremely evident that he knew what time of year it was.

Since Dandy was a ranch horse, he was kept in the pasture with the other ranch riding horses, all of which were mares. One of these was Cookie, the apricot-eating mare, always full of personality and seemingly always finding another way to surprise us. Cookie really liked to have her way in everything, and was the ruler of all the horses in the pasture, including Dandy. As spring rolled around, we noticed that Cookie was keeping between Dandy and the other mares. It was as if her special project was to make sure none of the other mares got near him, for any reason. As she worked to keep him from the other mares, she gave him so much attention that not even eating seemed as important as being in charge of him. She would sidle up to him, making small, romantic noises, and he began to notice her special attentions. Judy and I happened to be looking out at the pasture when, to our total astonishment, we saw Dandy mount Cookie and perform as a stallion would, then get off and go back to grazing contentedly. Cookie casually followed him, a look of satisfaction and success on her face. Had we not watched it happen, we would have probably doubted the triumph of seduction over surgery, but it was very real to all involved, and they repeated this lovemaking periodically over quite a lengthy time.

Now, an example of violence, to keep the Hollywood tradition alive.

One summer Bill invited another actor, James Woods, to visit the ranch, as he was considering getting a country place himself. He brought with him a classy, high-dollar looking girl friend and his dog, a Jack Russell terrier

Bill was not available that day to come to the ranch, so I played tour guide, showing them around the ranch a bit, then into the main barn. As we crossed from one stall to another, I glimpsed a flash of movement out of the corner of my eye, then all at once I heard a scream, and as I looked to see what was going on, the scream diminished into sobs, coming from Mr. Woods' girl friend. She was sobbing uncontrollably, hiding her face in his shoulder. He was at a loss as to what was going on, as he hadn't seen anything, same as me.

While he comforted her, I looked around the stall and found the cause of her problem. When we entered the stall to walk through, she had gone in first, with the terrier, and a barn cat was there. She was the only one that saw the dog instantaneously grab and kill the cat, setting off her scream. She was devastated; she probably had never seen that kind of carnage and had no idea it existed. I tried to let her know that there was nothing done wrong, and the dog wasn't to be blamed for doing what comes naturally, but it didn't seem to help.

Explaining that barn cats are expendable, replaceable, probably already replaced, didn't seem to help, either. She was ready to go back to Hollywood, right now, and wouldn't be comforted. They left soon after that, and my guess is that James Woods traded her off before he got a place in the country, if he ever did get one.

Again, to bow to the mores of Hollywood storytelling, I relate an incident of a love triangle.

Cookie remained in love with Dandy all the time she was at the ranch. When the breeding season came, we could count on her demanding that Dandy fulfill her longings, and he seemed happy (as well as capable) of obliging. Each year she took charge of his care and keeping, at least if that meant keeping him away from the other mares.

A new mare, Lady, another ranch riding horse, came to the ranch, so she was kept in the same group as Cookie. Dandy wanted to get acquainted with this lovely new mare, but Cookie kept getting in the way. It was comical to watch Cookie position herself between them. There wasn't a lot of violence or contention, just a body always there.

One spring morning Judy was watching out the window and realized Lady had come into heat. Now Lady really wanted to get to know Dandy, thinking of him as the local stallion, and kept working her way around Cookie to be near him. Dandy sensed a new feeling of excitement, and he started toward Lady. Cookie moved in between them, pinning her ears back and being really serious about keeping them apart. Again Dandy walked around Cookie, and again she pushed in between Dandy and Lady. This went on for some time, with Lady being kept well away from the increasingly interested Dandy.

The scene changed when Cookie apparently realized that Dandy wasn't getting what he wanted. It was as if Cookie looked seriously at Dandy and wanted him to have what he desired. Dandy started toward Lady again and Cookie just turned and walked away, as if to say, "Well, you may as well go to her, it looks like she's here to stay," and Dandy went to Lady, performed his quasi-stallion responsibility, then all three of them returned to grazing peacefully. Love (or Hollywood lust) wins again.

CHAPTER 43

―――――――――― ● ――――――――――

Screen Test

One summer day a large van followed Bill's Volvo to the ranch. Bill explained that he had a camera crew to do some shots of the ranch just in case they were needed in the future. They parked by the barn and set up to film at the corral above the barn, with the ranch house and the trees around it in the background.

It was enjoyable watching the crew set up, and to get not just cameras but also sound equipment ready. They had Bill get in the corral and talk to calibrate everything, and filmed him talking about how special the ranch is to him. I was sitting on the fence taking it all in, when Bill said, "Come over here." I climbed down into the corral and joined him, then he indicated for me to stay there and he went over by the camera man. From there he started asking me questions about the ranch, about Three Rivers, and then about horses.

Those who know horse people understand that talking about horses is our strong point, or weakness, depending on how you feel about pedigrees, and I raved on in detail about Doc Bar, Mr Gunsmoke, Old Granddad, Doc O Lena, Rey Jay (the famous one-eyed cutting horse) and others we hoped to include in the blood lines of our breeding program until Bill finally shut me down. I felt a little silly, thinking I had gone on and on instead of just answering his questions, but realized later that was what he had wanted. It wasn't until much later that I came to know it was actually an informal screen test to see if I had any potential for doing something more than manage a ranch. The answer apparently was "no" to what he had in mind, as nothing further was ever said or done. Looking back, that "no" was the best thing that could happen at that time, as my life was complicated enough without adding another dimension in a field in which I have zero knowledge. Nevertheless, I'll always be grateful that Bill had the consideration to make this effort; it is a good example of Bill's big heart and his desire to help others do the best they can with their lives. He is not just a celebrity, but is a real person with feelings and great love for those around him and apparently will do what is in his power to help others get ahead.

CHAPTER 44

•

Gifts from Bill

In the spring of 1980 Bill and Marcy traveled to New York City on film business, and while there toured an exhibit at the Metropolitan Museum of Art called "The Horses of San Marco," relating to the origins and glory of the famous sculptures in Venice. They were so impressed that before they left New York, Bill commissioned someone to professionally mount theatre-sized posters advertising the exhibit and send them to California: one for his house in Three Rivers, and one for us. These have a photographic reproduction of the two famous war horses in a majestic pose, and show off grandly these incredibly impressive works of art. We were so pleased to have one of these posters, and still have it hanging in our living room even though we are not living at Bill's ranch anymore. It has traveled many miles with us, and been proudly displayed in living areas as we lived in Idaho, Wyoming, and California.

Sometime in the early 1980s Bill asked if we ate steak. We said, "Not often, but we really enjoy it when we do!" He then informed us that on his next visit he and Marcy would bring steaks and we'd have dinner together. When the day arrived, they didn't drive up from LA as they usually did, but instead here came a big, white limousine slowly up the ranch road. Bill explained that he needed time to rest, so didn't want to drive. Also, it turned out, the limo driver was great at barbequing steaks. It was a wonderful dinner.

Not too long after that, Bill came to the ranch house with a box in hand. He explained that he had found the perfect door knocker for his house, and wanted us to have one too. We were astonished to see a several-inch tall bronze sculpture of the head and neck of a quarter horse, exceptionally well done, with a knocker made from a bronzed horse shoe. This treasure traveled with us when we left the ranch, and nearly thirty years later, when we determined it was never going to find a better place to reside, we gave it to Sal Natoli, the present ranch manager, receiving the promise that it would be permanently mounted at the front door to the ranch house.

My son, Chris, wanted something to remember Bill by when we left the ranch. That summer Bill came to the ranch for a weekend trip, and Chris went down to Bill's house to visit. He returned beaming, grinning from ear to ear. When he asked Bill for a remembrance Bill brought out an 8x10 photo of himself and after quite a bit of thought autographed it "For Chris—My Partner." There could not have been, to Chris, a more meaningful gesture.

The point of telling of these gifts is to reiterate Bill's generous nature. He truly cares about people and is thoughtful and kind. Sometimes the television images he portrays are about anything but that, but remember he is following someone's direction. We still feel that the real Bill is a good human, and we enjoyed our time associating with him.

CHAPTER 45

◉

Beginning of the End

We had been at the ranch several years and things had turned around in the horse business. The cycle had shifted from one of high prices at sales to an atmosphere of "how can we sell something, anything, to bring in some income?" In order for the IRS to stand still for the seemingly endless losses that a horse operation can generate, the ranch must produce a profit occasionally. This became really difficult in that time of tight horse sales and low prices on those that did sell, except in the very top quality (or most popular) lines of horses, including those we owned.

The real estate office I had established in Three Rivers, in combination with the ALW business, was producing a living, but not a sumptuous one. I was happy to receive the proceeds from any transaction, since the horse operation was not only not profitable, but had no promise of ever being so with the market such as it had become in our "good, but not top-of-the-line" horses.

One day Victor called from the business office and asked if I thought it was possible to sell the thirty acres we had acquired a few years earlier. Land prices had appreciated remarkably in Three Rivers, I told him, and I felt confident the acreage would sell at a price significantly higher than they had paid for it, but it had become such an integral part of the ranch operation that I hated to see it go. Also, it still was one of the really desirable properties on the South Fork, with gentle slopes, good new fences, an excellent stand of permanent pasture grass, and ample irrigation water from the extension of the gravity-flow system. Those in the business of ranching don't sell that kind of property. He listened, but when I hung up I felt that in the overall scheme of things he had some motivation other than just horse ranching, or at least horse ranching in Three Rivers. We had learned that Bill and Marcy had purchased a ranch in Kentucky for their Saddlebred operation and named it the Belle Reve Farm, and we expected that also was a factor in reducing the size of the Belle Reve Ranch. We were still naïve enough to be offended that Bill, apparently motivated mostly by Marcy's urgings, had chosen to put his major horse investments in Saddlebreds, including an expensive stallion, and in the Kentucky farm instead of the business that would benefit us. It seemed to us that our agreement to build a horse business in the informal "partnership" we had begun with was no longer important to anyone but us, as the ranch and the quarter horses seemed to become less and less a priority in Bill's mind and actions.

It wasn't long before Victor asked if I would find a buyer for the thirty acres, apparently what he considered to be a surplus property, and my assumption was that a sale of some property at a large gain would allow the ranch to show the IRS that a profit could be produced. The trouble with that, I realized, was that if the business office could satisfy the IRS needs for profit through other means than gains in the horse operation, then there was probably no way that Judy and I would ever see a share of a profitable operation even when the horse business turned around, which was what our original agreement had been based on. This realization had nagged at my feelings for some time, but the real problem showed up a little later when we had a chance to sell the property.

One of the first rules a real estate broker learns is to get everything in writing, but since we had worked on a very close, personal basis with this office for several years I went ahead without a written brokerage contract and quietly offered the east thirty acres for sale. Almost immediately we stimulated the interest of a capable buyer from our existing real estate client list that made an offer, and I sent the offer to Victor. Acceptable price and terms were negotiated, and the property went under contract of sale.

As closing approached, I called Victor to discuss adding to the escrow instructions the arrangements for a commission on the sale. After all, I was a licensed broker, I had found a buyer and negotiated a contract, and closing was approaching. To my complete amazement, Victor said the business office was not authorizing a commission to be paid to me. As I protested, all he would say was, "We'll take care of you." I repeated my request for a commission for my efforts, and he repeated, "We'll take care of you."

I did not, and still do not, know exactly what he meant by that phrase. The concept of being "taken care of" is not what the entrepreneurial mind is looking for when completing an earned transaction. I couldn't fathom the mindset that would not pay my brokerage a commission for the performance of what had been requested, especially in view of the significant profit on the sale of the property. I discussed with Judy not just the fact that we were not getting paid for this transaction, but that I felt the business office was not seeing my side of our conversation. Probably I should have made a bigger effort to get Victor to understand my feelings. Perhaps I should have been sharing with him all along how tenuous our personal situation was so he would appreciate how important it was to me to have that income, but that was never a comfortable thing to consider, as it would point out my failings as a provider for my family and my apparent short-sightedness in setting up our original agreement on caring for the ranch. Looking back now, I see it was to my detriment that I didn't communicate better with Victor, because he had always been fair with us. Too late,

I realized a more satisfactory answer could have come from an open conversation all along about these things.

I think the way this was handled, along with the realization that we were never included in any thinking regarding showing a profit to divide as our original understanding had been, was instrumental in us becoming motivated to leave the ranch not long after that. Again, I am at fault for not pressing the business office to perform, or at the very least to discuss, what I was thinking should have been considered, when in the overall scheme of things the ranch was not the most important part of Bill's financial arrangements, or even by this time, not the most important part of his growing horse business.

Two other factors constantly entered into my thinking at this time. The real estate office was showing promise again, and the ALW business was in the surge mode. I had acquired a mobile phone, one of the early "bag phone" varieties, as that let me keep in touch with business on the road between Three Rivers and Visalia. This was 1984, and I was one of the few that had a phone in my car. I was working harder and longer, hopefully combined with smarter, and was seeing some progress. I thought that the time for us to leave the ranch and its demands was probably approaching, but not quite there. We would hang on a little longer.

CHAPTER 46

•

The Final Chapter

As time progressed, it became evident that Judy and I were not accomplishing what we needed to raise our family. As earlier stated, we were being adequately compensated by the ranch for caretaking, with extra pay for construction or other special projects, but it wasn't what we needed to live on, and the condition of the horse market was such that there was no promise of ever seeing a significant profit from the sale of quarter horses. Spending the time it takes to run a horse operation detracted seriously from my other business ventures. The nature of self-employment is that it is very demanding of personal time and mental energy. What had seemed like a good idea some years earlier was obviously not working as planned. We had spent enough time for the combination of businesses we had embraced to work, if it was going to.

Judy and I discussed our options. The association with Bill was enjoyable but had no promise of ever being profitable financially for our family. Our girls were now gone, though their needs were still demanding of us as parents, and my other kids, living out of state and visiting the ranch in summers, seemed totally neglected because I was so tied down with the demands of the ranch and keeping our other businesses going to try to earn a living.

For all these reasons we determined it was time to leave the ranch. It will always be a special time and place to us and to our family, and as I write this we have returned to Three Rivers and live just across the river, still share the same swimming hole, ride some of the same trails we rode then, and enjoy the unequalled ambiance of these special foothills of the Sierra. We look across at the lush, green pastures of the ranch and see the irrigation system still working, the road and general ranch layout to be unchanged and still satisfactory, and think what a great thing to have been able to be counted as a guiding force in this. How blessed we have been to have these extraordinary experiences, and to get to know the personalities of those with whom we have spent time.

We have not reestablished a relationship with Bill, but still follow his career moves as he continues, even in advancing years, to thrill many fans with his abilities and talents. May he continue to enjoy the Belle Reve Ranch as long as he lives, and may his family continue that legacy.

EPILOGUE

◉

How do I feel about my time spent with the rich and famous? It was a period of life that I have many fond memories of, and a few not so pleasant. In other words, it was part of life. I did learn some things about myself, one being that there is nothing about being rich and/or famous that is attractive enough to trade my loving family life for it. Undoubtedly the most important lesson was that regardless of the seeming strength of the stresses of life, prioritizing to keep love and relationships at the top of the heart's values will guide us through any trials. I appreciate the good things I know about Bill's relationship with his kids and grandkids and applaud him for maintaining those relationships.

Recently I spent some time with Grant, a grandson of Bill, and another neighbor moving an unwanted driftwood log that winter floods had left in the swimming hole. As the three of us labored together while being watched by some locals and some Southern California friends of Grant, I realized that this is part of the magic of Three Rivers, that some who live the Hollywood life style and some who are content to be totally away from the limelight can come together with no need for pretense or show to accomplish a project. Nobody needs to do certain things to impress someone else; everyone is welcomed for what they are. The spirit of these mountains and rivers influences for good all that put themselves in tune with that quiet place of the heart.

The South Fork of Three Rivers is not a place for a commercialized horse ranch or other worldly business venture, but a place to build hearts full of love and togetherness. This magic simply requires time to let it become part of each person who is exposed to it.

I am one of the lucky ones. I realized early on that the spirit of this special place can bring peace to minds and hearts, but I had the advantage of the most wonderful teacher. Judy's love reached into the depths of my soul and taught it how to respond to love, and how to recognize deep feelings I didn't know existed. Then, through all the financial and other trials that my sometimes less-than-sagacious decisions brought, she kept loving me, and if there are beneficial life lessons to the reader of this saga, they are to her credit. She made it possible for our relationship to not just continue, but to grow and flourish through these trials, and because of her love, my life bloomed. I thank her for all those wonderful feelings I have had over the years and still enjoy all the time that we are together.

The magic of Three Rivers brings us a better understanding of and appreciation for all those we meet in life. As I met some Hollywood figures and also got acquainted with various people in the horse business I recognized personality types that I had met before both in the corporate world and in my later self-employment times, both positive and negative. Humans will always be the most interesting creatures on earth, and some, like William Shatner, have filled my thoughts with many hours of entertainment. He is an entertainer, after all.

APPENDIX A

—————— • ——————

Excerpted, by permission, from Quarter Horse Of The Pacific Coast, March, 1982.

BELLE REVE RANCH—THE BEAUTIFUL DREAM

By Jill Scopinich

The horse in the adjacent sale ring holds no interest for you. With the auctioneer's cadence becoming a drone in your ears, you find yourself bored and a little sleepy. To break the boredom, you scan the audience. Mostly horsemen, dressed western-style. A few pretty girls, but they all seem to be accompanied by great, big men. Better not gaze too long at one of them or you're apt to leave the sale real fast—and not by your own choice.

You keep your eyes moving. Suddenly you spot someone who looks very familiar. He's wearing a western hat and the brim casts a shadow on the face. Who is it? A horseman you've done business with before? No. Someone you met at another sale? No. Gradually it sinks in. 'Why, he looks like...no, it couldn't be, not here at a Quarter Horse sale. Must be my imagination.'

Think again. It not only could be, it probably was William Shatner, the actor who, as Captain Kirk, rode his way to stardom on the spaceship Enterprise in the hit television series Star Trek.

Shatner is the latest in his profession to join the ranks of Quarter

150

Horse owners and breeders. He and his wife, Marci, together with Dalan and Judy Smith, are rapidly nearing their goal of developing their Belle Reve Ranch into an establishment that symbolizes the finest in cutting horse breeding.

Located in the small town of Three Rivers, California, the ranch encompasses 20 acres, two houses and several outbuildings. The emphasis at Belle Reve, as it appears to be in Shatner's life in general, is on quality rather than quantity. Their ranch is small enough to allow total control, yet large enough that everyone involved may take an active role in its operation. Optimally, they hope to keep the horse population to 16 although they could, if necessary, expand to 20 without feeling crowded.

Shatner has played many roles in his career, but none he has enjoyed as much or taken as seriously as that of a family man. It was partly due to his devotion to his wife and three children that Belle Reve (which means beautiful dream in French) was born. "I think that a family that has mutual interests that grow as the children grow—like horses, riding and the outdoors—shares more," Shatner emphasizes. "It's longer lasting than a birthday party or an outing at an amusement park. Taking care of a horse is a major job for a child and I think children of any age learn a great deal when they have the responsibility of a live animal."

In addition to breeding and raising high-quality cutting horses, Shatner and Smith have embarked on a new project. Aptly named 'The Stock Market,' their new service is designed to unite those with horses to sell with those who are looking to buy. They act as a clearinghouse of sorts, matching the abilities of the horse for sale with needs of prospective buyers.

In his business world, an actor is surrounded by fantasy and dreams. In his private world, however, he is subject to the harsh realities of everyday life. The constant traverse from fantasy to reality can have a debilitating effect on some, but not on Shatner. For he has managed to do what most of us can only hope to do. He has combined the best of both worlds with his Belle Reve Ranch.

Last November, I had the fortunate opportunity to interview William Shatner when he and Dalan Smith were in Sacramento to attend the Pacific Coast Cutting Futurity Sale. Following is our conversation:

Quarter Horse: When did you become interested in horses and how did that interest develop?

Shatner: When I lived in Montreal, Canada, about half a mile away there was a horse rental place—where you could ride in the muddy fields. I used to go there and swab out the stables. For that I got to ride the horses. So as a kid of about 10 or 12, I was a country boy in the big city.

And I grew up spending a great deal of time in the mountains that are about 90 miles east of Montreal. I spent summers there and worked as a counselor in all kinds of camps for underprivileged kids. I taught hiking, woodworking and horseback riding, as well as drama. So my interest in animals and horses was developed in Canada in those early years.

I always fancied myself as a horseman, but I never had enough instructional practice. It was only when I got to Hollywood and they wanted me to do westerns that I really had to learn how to ride. Sometimes I would be in a cavalry picture and I had to have a good seat like a cavalry officer. Other times they would be cowboy movies and I would have to sit in that relaxed fashion and yet be part of the horse. But the thing that really got me perfected, to the degree that I became perfected, was a pilot for a series that I made that became a motion picture based on the life of Alexander the Great. Alexander and his troops rode without saddles, so I had to ride bareback. And I rode the five-gaited champion of southern California—whose name, I think, was King—bareback! I had to learn dressage bareback, and even learn to post bareback!

Quarter Horse: And you stayed on?

Shatner: Not only did I stay on, I had to do tricks with him, I had to rear him!

One time about three or four years prior to this a horse reared on me unexpectedly and, not having had any training, I did the one thing you are not supposed to do—I held onto the reins and pulled back. I pulled the horse back on me. I can vividly recollect this horse slowly going back and my thinking, 'Good Lord, is this really going to happen?' then the sudden visions and memory of having read about men being crushed underneath the horse! As the horse came back and back, suddenly I was staring at the sky. At the last instant the horse fell on his side, so my leg was under him. Luckily, the ground was soft so I only had a bruise from knee to thigh and I was able to recover from that in a few weeks.

Now, having been traumatized by that, I had to rear the horse bareback without the ability to hold on to the pommel and without the brace of the stirrups. The cue for this horse was a pull on the mane. You would hold the reins with the left hand, give him the cue with the right hand and he would rear. The man who trained the horses for Ben Hur trained this horse and was also training me to ride him.

I also had to mount this horse bareback, in a regal fashion, with a cloak like the Greeks wore! So this all became part of my training. I trained for nine months.

I think it was as a result of that that my desire to own my own horses came about. When I married my wife, Marci, we shared a mutual interest in horses. We used to go riding with my kids as often as possible. We would rent horses in the Los Angeles area.

Quarter Horse: What made you decide to buy a ranch?

Shatner: We had decided we needed to find a place outside of

Los Angeles because of the smog, the heat and our desire for country living. About a year before this, I had been doing some work for the town of Visalia for a Shakespeare festival. They had asked me to come up and help them raise money for an artistic project. Because of my background as a Shakespearian actor I was really interested in making this project work. So, three or for times I visited the town of Visalia. I had never been there before. While I was there I met some people who lived in Three Rivers and they said it was 'heaven on earth.'

A year later my wife and I were looking for a place to invest in and get away to, and we were thinking of somewhere on the ocean. So we started driving up the coast. We drove past Hearst Castle and the property values were just extraordinary—it was impossible to find anything within the range of what we wanted to spend.

Suddenly we remembered what we had heard about Three Rivers and thought, 'Why even look on the beach when we could go inland and combine horses with our plans?' So we drove to Three Rivers that very day.

It was Sunday and all the real estate offices were closed. But I saw one office which was a home and office combined. A woman drove up to it—she was probably coming home from church—and I ran across the street and snagged her. I said, "I know you're closed, but we are up here for only a few hours. We are real, live customers, we're not 'Lookie Lous'" and that clinched it.

We described the requirements we had for the property and she said she knew of only one place in the area that had exactly what we were looking for. She took us to this property and into our lives fell Dalan Smith, who was our answer from heaven, if you will. He was looking for the very same things we were looking for—a ranch, horses, management. He was seeking to settle in Three Rivers with his family. We met and combined in a partnership and he is in business in Three Rivers and in business with me.

Quarter Horse: What was the property like when you bought it?

Shatner: There was a house, a good house, but (the land) had lain fallow since it had been cultivated. There were no fences, no livestock and the grass was as high as my shoulders. As we were walking around looking at it the agent told us to be careful of rattlesnakes!

Since then we have fenced it, added irrigation, brought livestock in and the fields have been sown for better quality grass. The property is 20 acres with a river running through it, so we built a house on the river. Now there are two houses on the property.

Quarter Horse: Why did you name the ranch Belle Reve?

Shatner: Belle Reve is French for beautiful dream. And it is Marci's and my dream to have horses and a place by the water. It is our dream house. It also has been our dream to have friends who have that interest as well. Now, out of the Visalia-Three Rivers area, we have made friends with people in the Shakespearian festival, which, unfortunately, has moved on to the Fresno area, and those in the Three Rivers area who have horses and cattle.

Quarter Horse: How much time do you spend at the ranch?

Shatner: We have been there as frequently as weekly and we have left gaps as long as months. I (was) shooting the movie Star Trek II, so I haven't been there in a couple of months. Now that I'm finished, I'll go up next week and plan a schedule.

A pilot for a series called Hooker that I made recently will be on as a replacement late this spring, and my life will have a certain order to it that it didn't have when I was working on a free-lance basis. So I am planning to go up every weekend.

Quarter Horse: Why did you choose to breed cutting horses?

Shatner: The original reason for choosing cutting horses was mainly due to a conversation with Dalan in which we talked about what we wished to do.

We breed dogs as well—Dobermans. In fact, my lack of knowledge of the conformation of horses is lessened by my knowledge of the conformation of Dobermans. They are not dissimilar. The dog action, the stance and even the terminology—the breadth of chest, the look in the horse's eyes and the look in the Doberman's eyes, the spirit of each, is just as important as conformation.

It seems my life has been blessed with people who have come into my life and taught me things I would not have known otherwise. The first one, and certainly a major force, has been my wife, Marci, who although I introduced her to Dobermans, (has) introduced me to the breeding of Dobermans and the pure esthetics of Dobermans.

In the same way, I have always admired Quarter Horses, which I rode in movies. But the esthetics of Quarter Horses are being taught to me by the Smiths and I'm a willing student. I have much to learn. I'm only a rank amateur, but the process of learning is just as enjoyable as the breeding and the acquisition of horses.

Quarter Horse: Have you been studying bloodlines?

Shatner: I'm studying everything. That's why I read your magazine, and read it religiously. I don't take the magazine, look at a few ads, read an article and throw it in a pile somewhere. I go from cover to cover, right to the end of the want ads to see who's advertising and how much they're going for! It's difficult to keep in mind what those foundation lines are, who is being bred to whom, what is selling, if a month or two months go by when you have last talked about it.

It's like trying to remember a friend's kid's name! I think of myself as a dummy when I can't quite remember who is being bred to whom and I have to ask again, when Dalan has already told me seven times during the year! But I've also had to remember a number of lines—certain number of words—ten pages a day during that time! So I learn the horses' names and bloodlines very quickly for the weekend and then it goes out of my mind on Monday! I'm hoping everybody's like that, or else they'll say, 'Here comes dummy Shatner—he's going to ask me about that horse again!'

Quarter Horse: I don't think you're alone! Who makes the major decisions regarding the acquisition of horses for the ranch?

Shatner: We share it, based on his information and my income!

Quarter Horse: I like Dalan's end of it best!

Shatner: Well they're both acquired with great difficulty, let me tell you!

Quarter Horse: What bloodlines are you concentrating on now?

Shatner: Let me take a shot at that and Dalan can elaborate. We are trying to diversify, so we have King breeding (and) we're breeding to Doc Bar sons. We also have Leo bloodlines.

Dalan Smith: We have one Dart Bar mare that's being bred in the Freckles line. We think this will produce an excellent cross. She's a wonderful mare, with that Three Bars fire. She's by Doc's Drift Bar out of a Dart Bar mare, by Three Bars, so she's got Three Bars (through) Dart Bar and Three bars on the bottom side, also. So, by breeding her to the Freckles line, we figure the Three Bars end will bring in enough fire and the Freckles line will bring in the cow, so that should be a fine baby!

Shatner: It is obvious Dalan is the brains behind the operation and I am trying to learn from him. We are experimenting with the breeding lines we're talking about to bring about a new bloodline that people have not thought of or haven't had the opportunity to try.

Quarter Horse: How many mares do you now have?

Shatner: We have six. And we may keep some of our fillies. We have some two-year-olds for sale, we have a great gelding who has been lauded by the trainer as one of the best horses he has trained, we have some outstanding fillies.

For example, we have (Miss) Sheila Bay, who has produced some outstanding foals.

Smith: Sheila Bay is basic King breeding. She's by Rocky Knox by

Rock Springs by King. On the bottom side she's Starduster bred. She's a very refined mare and puts that look on all of her babies. Her oldest foal is by Poco Tivio. His name is Bronc Tivio and he sold last fall for $30,000 and went back East. We have a Montana Doc yearling out of her. This spring she is being bred to Mr Gunsmoke.

Shatner: Speaking of Mr Gunsmoke, Gary Wexler (Mr Gunsmoke's owner) is a name I would like to mention. He has been a great influence on Dalan and me. Although he is fairly new to the horse business, he has been a pillar of strength to us.

I read an article in your magazine about Wexler's sale that I thought was excellent. It was a fair and righteous article that described exactly the way I felt about the sale. It was a wonderful event—it worked. What fun it was to wear a black tie and to avoid stepping on horse droppings! It was fun and I'll go back just because it was fun!

Smith: We also have a two-year-old by Broadway Doc out of Sheila Bay, a Dry Doc filly out of a Gunsmoke mare and a gelding by Doc Tom Tucker, among others.

Shatner: Another name I would like to mention, in relation to cutting and training, is Will Landers, who has been doing a fine job of training our two-year-olds. I think he's an up-and-coming trainer. It is my hope to work with him and learn enough about riding cutting horses so that I may ride.

Smith: Our next broodmare may be a well-trained cutting horse that Bill can spend some time on. We'll raise babies in between.

Quarter Horse: Do you ever plan to buy and stand a stallion of your own on your ranch?

Shatner: I have a nine-month-old Doberman puppy who weighs 70 pounds and is only half grown. Just controlling him, especially when a female dog in heat comes by, is nearly impossible! Imagine a 1,500-pound stallion becoming uncontrollable! It would be overwhelming!

We would need to increase the size of our operation and have someone completely responsible for that end of it. It certainly would be a 'Belle Reve' to have our own stallion and bring our mares and a selected few outside mares to him. But it's a larger operation than we envision at the moment.

Besides which, the idea of crossing our mares with different stallions is really what we are into at the moment.

Our plans are to keep increasing the quality of the Belle Reve Ranch to where it becomes known that when our babies come up for sale, our ranch's name will be the standard of quality. People, when they buy from us, will know they will get a quality colt or filly that the Belle Reve name will stand behind.

Quarter Horse: At what point do you intend to sell your foals—before or after they are trained?

Shatner: We have still not determined that. If the foal is really exceptional we will keep it and train it, and perhaps we'll even campaign one in a year or two. This year we sold a couple of two-year-olds and we'll probably sell a yearling. But generally, we'll put a little training on them and sell them a two-year-olds.

Quarter Horse: What is the ultimate goal of the ranch?

Shatner: The goal of the ranch is to have the highest quality horses coming out on a regular basis, in a small but steady stream. Looking at our stock now, it's terrific. But we want to go even further.

Quarter Horse: Do you attend many horse events?

Shatner: Our operation is just three years old and it took me some time to become accustomed to the idea of buying and selling at these prices! So we started slowly. Now I'm beginning to understand more implicitly what's involved in buying and selling horses.

The tradition we (are) following—what the bloodlines are, what mares are good, what pepper and salt we should add to the soup of breeding—that is the beauty of it. Can we get that mare and then cross that mare with that stallion. Then it becomes a search for the right mare in the right price range. Then we wonder if we can go to a sale and pick up a mare more cheaply at auction than we can through the seller. Now the intricacies of buying and selling become a chess game, the intrigue of which I did not appreciate until recently. Now I'm totally involved!

Quarter Horse: You have many fans among horse people. How do they react when they see you at your ranch or the horse events you attend?

Shatner: The recognition factor as an actor is momentary. Then, a horse dealer is a horse dealer and the conversation becomes based on the quality of our horses.

Quarter Horse: Is there a difference between horsepeople and those you meet in show business?

Shatner: It seems to me that there is a certain kind of person I am attracted to. What they do in life has nothing to do with why I'm attracted to them. I think the basic attraction (for me) is a down-to-earth, straightforward person who is attracted to basic qualities of life (and) that the social amenities are meaningless to. There are certain things in life that are important and it is the people who value those things that I am attracted to.

The things that are important are love, family and (the) traditional qualities which those represent—that attracts me. The dilettantes and the people who are (phony), in any field, whether they are horsemen or actors, do not.

Quarter Horse: It seems as if many famous people are involved in Quarter Horses. Robert Redford has cutting horses, Robert Mitchum and Doc Severinson have running Quarter Horses, etc. Why do you think this is so?

Shatner: I don't know, except everyone you have mentioned there has done westerns. I don't think their backgrounds are western or ranching. It's possible that, in doing western movies they became acquainted with horses the same way I did.

Horses are a mystical creature, anyway. They have a spirit or mystique about them that goes back to our beginnings. I love physical contact with a horse. I love to physically put my hands on a horse. I have driven up to the ranch from Los Angeles and back in a day just to see a newborn foal. Seven hours of driving just to see a baby! I have wanted to get there to see the birth of a baby. I haven't yet been able to time it right—they don't give us any warning. There's a physicality about a horse. Especially the Quarter Horse. That head, those eyes, that body—they're beautiful!

At Wexler's sale one of those young studs was up for sale and he looked at me, and I looked at him, and I fell in love with him. He was sold to somebody else. But when I looked at those eyes I couldn't get the vision of him out of my head! This is crazy, but that horse will always be with me, because he was mystically beautiful. In fact, the imprint of that horse in my mind will be the template for all the horses we breed. I would like all our horses to look like that and have that feeling about them. And if they don't meet the standard, they're less.

If that stallion had been a mare, I'd have bought her. If I ever see a mare that looks at me that way, and I'm working, I'll buy her!

Quarter Horse: You seem to be going through a transition period right now. Where are you headed?

Shatner: That's an interesting comment. Up to now, I have had to deal with the responsibilities of bringing up a family. My thinking was always oriented towards how a decision would affect the family. I couldn't go on tour, I couldn't go to New York, and if a movie required me to go on location for a period of time, I had to think about whether I could go or not. Now my children are grown and I am in a transition. My wife and I are free again. We can do things we want to do and the ranch is one of them. So it is a period of transition—artistically and socially and domestically.

Quarter Horse: Ten years from now, what will you be doing?

Shatner: I'll be in a cutting event, trying to get a ROM!

Quarter Horse: Has it ever occurred to you that the character of Captain Kirk of Star Trek is like a pioneer wagonmaster?

Shatner: There's a great deal of thought that the origination of Captain Kirk and Star Trek was Wagon Train. It was deliberately based on the Forrester books of Captain Horatio Hornblower. But Wagon Train is also back there somewhere. He (Kirk) is very much the wagonmaster, leading his pioneer group to new frontiers. Instead of riding a horse, he rides the Enterprise.

I am a licensed pilot, and when you train as a pilot, and this goes back to the story I was telling you about rearing, you train with power on, power off stalls. You go up into a stall and correct. When I was trained as a pilot I kept thinking there was something vaguely familiar about the feeling of going up and coming back down. I was freaked out from the beginning, as all junior pilots are, about the stall maneuver. But then finally I realized what it was. Flying and riding, especially flying a glider, which I'm checked out on as well, is very similar. You fly by the seat of your pants. The instruments just tell you when you hit a thermal.

I love the use of nature in whatever I'm doing. Horseback riding, archery, which I enjoy, I love to sail and I ski extremely well. I love the use of the natural forces. Riding a horse, the balance, the oneness with the horse, the horse's unity with the earth is all part of the unity of nature. The ranch and land are even part of the unity of nature.

One evening, Marci and I sat out on the balcony of our home—we're surrounded by hills—and all we did was watch the sun go down and feel the natural rhythm that you forget in the city. The sun rising, reaching its zenith and falling. The animals, both wild and domesticated, all follow that pattern. One forgets that that is the natural sequence. You get into a false order in the city, so you have to be reminded every so often of what is real.

The city is as necessary as the country. It represents the apotheosis of civilization. The city is art and philosophy and the progression of man's social world. But you can get into an ivory tower there and forget your roots. So I think a balance is necessary.

Quarter Horse: I cannot conclude this interview without asking this question. Will they really kill Mr. Spock in Star Trek III?

Shatner: In science fiction, nothing is permanent.

ABOUT THE AUTHOR

Dalan Smith, oldest boy of nine children, grew up on a small farm and went to grade school in a two-room schoolhouse in southeastern Idaho, where he learned how to work hard and create a lot of his own entertainment. The rural community was home for several other families of loving relatives and practical jokers, which taught him the importance of learning from quiet observation and to seize opportunities for sweet seclusion in the form of fly fishing or duck hunting along the river's edge.

After serving a mission for his church, early university studies were on a scientific track, then were switched to business when his interest in motivating people became more fascinating than researching scientific principles.

Dalan was never one to follow the crowd, and these entrepreneurial ways led to nearly five decades of primarily self-employment in real estate and construction. During these years he emphasized to his agents and employees the development of their talents and self-esteem by choosing options with the most benefits to the customer or client, rather than the most money to the agent in the short term.

Dalan and his wife, Judy, live happily in Three Rivers, California, where his continuing efforts to encourage those around him are directed primarily through his church and supplemented with occasional mailings to those he "adopts."

CPSIA information can be obtained
at www.ICGtesting.com
Printed in the USA
BVHW041922120520
579592BV00010B/359

9 781469 960838